ONE BLOCK =
Many Quilts

ONE BLOCK
=
Many Quilts

Agnete Kay

American Quilter's Society
P. O. Box 3290 • Paducah, KY 42002-3290

Located in Paducah, Kentucky, the American Quilter's Society (AQS) is dedicated to promoting the accomplishments of today's quilters. Through its publications and events, AQS strives to honor today's quiltmakers and their work and to inspire future creativity and innovation in quiltmaking.

EDITOR: BARBARA SMITH

BOOK DESIGN/ILLUSTRATIONS: ELAINE WILSON AND ANGELA SCHADE

COVER DESIGN: MICHAEL BUCKINGHAM

PHOTOGRAPHY: CHARLES R. LYNCH

Library of Congress Cataloging-in-Publication Data

Kay, Agnete

    One block = many quilts / Agnete Kay

      p.   cm.

    ISBN 1-57432-719-4

      1. Patchwork--Patterns.   2. Quilting--Patterns.   I. Title.

TT835.K39   1999

746.46'041--dc21   98-51824

                                    CIP

Additional copies of this book may be ordered from the American Quilter's Society, PO Box 3290, Paducah, KY 42002-3290 @ $18.95. Add $2.00 for postage and handling.

Printed in the U.S.A. by Image Graphics, Paducah, KY

CONTENTS

DEDICATION

To our daughter Joanne,
who, when she first moved out
to share an apartment with a friend,
though happy, exclaimed woefully,
". . . but I'll be missing all these quilts!"

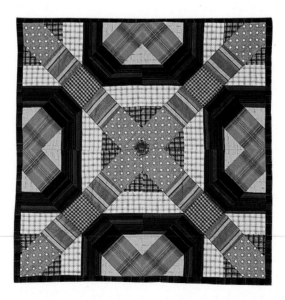

CABIN QUILT, 38½" x 38½", 1995, by the author.

ACKNOWLEDGMENTS

In addition to my inimitable family and friends,

editors and designers, sine qua non,

I want to thank Jurgen Gothe,

Frederic Raphael,

and Jim Carrey,

who all brightened my pathway awhile.

EASTERN BLOCKS, 29" x 40", 1997, by the author.

AQUARELLE I, 45" x 57½", 1995, by the author. For my first aquarelle (watercolor) quilt of mysterious plants and wildlife behind a trellis, I combined a brightly colored madras plaid and floral prints. The choices for setting the 12 finished blocks are almost limitless.

INTRODUCTION

In the craft store where I buy perle cotton for hand quilting, a lady said to me, "I wish I could make quilts. I wish I had the patience." I replied, "Well, you see, we don't do it because we are patient. We do it because it is exciting." She said, "But it's so hard. It's all mathematics. I can't do math." "Yes," I admitted. "There is a bit of math. Basically, you have to be able to tell the difference between a triangle and a square. If you can do that, you're all right." She laughed and I laughed, and I hope I convinced her that quiltmaking can be easy and exciting at the same time. I hope I will convince you, too.

I also want to show you how your stylistic choices and arrangements can give your quilt a look that places it and you in another place, another time. I will try to pin down some of the elements of style, however elusive. To be sure, our results will be pastiches, collages of bits and pieces. Pastiches can be boring imitations, or they can be witty or satirical. Successful or not, we learn and progress while making them.

While I was trying to design the ideal block for exploring the elements of style, it occurred to me that many books deal with color, value, design, or techniques, but few get into the topic of style. If they do, they equate it with history or geography, something that can be copied. I set out to make quilts that adopt, by easy means, certain styles of another age or place, but which are not copies. To my surprise and delight, I found it was possible to achieve what I was hoping for by using just one simple block.

Of course, whatever pattern you design, you can never be sure that someone, somewhere, has not drafted the same block, but at least I have never seen this block elsewhere. It is always quite possible that several people have thought of the same thing at once. Indeed, it happens surprisingly often. So, maybe the general contents of this book have been pondered by many quilters in their own ways. If so, my warmest greetings to you, I have not knowingly borrowed any ideas.

I call this new, versatile block the IMAGINE BLOCK because I like to travel in my imagination to any place in the world and choose fabrics of a pattern and style associated with that place, or I can travel in time to days gone by and choose fabric combinations in the styles and settings of yesteryear.

From 1994 to 1997, I made a score or more of very different quilts with this block. In some of the quilts, I used simple borders. Others have simple appliquéd features, some have sashing, some have plain setting squares, but only the IMAGINE BLOCK was used. It is these quilts I have chosen to feature in this book.

In accordance with my own preferences, none of these quilts was rotary-cut, strip-pieced, or computer-generated, and their construction was not particularly new and fast. Each one was hand-designed, hand-traced, scissors-cut, and machine-sewn. Many new time-saving techniques seem to me so cumbersome.

My method for making templates can be used for any quilt. There is geometry in these quilts; not geometric formulas, but geometry of the eye and mind, the play with points, lines, angles, and surfaces. Neither calculator nor computer is necessary. They dominate the job world today, so why not try to be without them in our leisure time?

It is expected that you are somewhat familiar with a pencil, paper, see-through ruler, pins, needles, thimble (if desired), good scissors, a sewing machine (I do not hand piece), an iron, and good humor. Formal qualifications are not necessary, but the basic sums and times tables, which we were obliged to learn by heart in school in the olden days, can be useful.

Some block and quilt patterns are provided, but I hope that, after you have read this book, you will agree that it is more fun to create your own blocks, now that you know how easy it is, and that you will be inspired to take your own imaginative journey.

CHAPTER 1

The *Imagine* Block

*I*f there is one thing that strikes me about Japanese quilts, apart from their incredible workmanship, it is the union of excitement and calm in one. I have tried, often and usually in vain, to achieve that exciting calm.

I like to make quilts the old-fashioned way, not missing out on the most interesting part: the earliest stages of the development of an idea. I like the satisfaction of drawing my very own lines on paper and cardboard, deciding which fabrics to use for which patches, and then placing my templates on the printed fabric exactly where I want, thereby enhancing the look of the finished block. Also, I like the feel and sound of good scissors cutting the fabric in resonance with the table top. This method, contrary to popular opinion, is not really very slow. In two hours, three medium-sized blocks can be traced, cut, and machine pieced, even allowing for a coffee break.

I make templates from cardboard, and many of my quilts have blocks that are 8½" x 8½" because I frequently use the cardboard backings from standard 8½" x 11" writing pads. You can also use poster board. Even cereal boxes or extra-large birthday cards are good. Maybe best of all are the "Would-you-like-a-box?" kind of boxes they give you at clothing stores, which make good template material.

Drawing the Block

To draw your first IMAGINE BLOCK on template material, you can begin with a square that is 8½" x 8½". If you are working with metric measurements, start with a 24 cm x 24 cm square. Using the metric system does not mean having to deal with strange numbers and fractions. It just means working with other, different sets of easy numbers.

Step by step

- With a sharp pencil and a see-through ruler, draw the four sides of an 8½" x 8½" square on template material. Use the corner of a piece of writing paper to check that your drawn corners are right angles. To test the rightness of the square, measure all four sides of the block to make sure they are the same length. Alternatively, you can measure both diagonals, which should be equal.

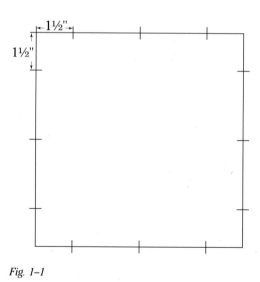

Fig. 1–1

- On your template square, mark the half-way point on each side. Then mark each side 1½" (3.75 cm) in from each corner (Fig. 1–1).

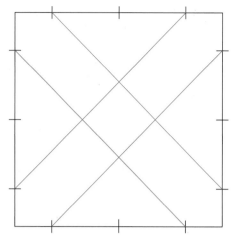

Fig. 1–2

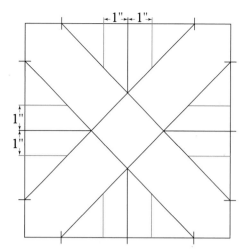

Fig. 1–4

- Draw diagonal lines from the marks near the corners to the marks at the opposite corners. You will be drawing two diagonal bands with a center square (Fig. 1–2).

- On both sides of the center line, draw lines 1" (2.5 cm) from and parallel to the center lines. Stop when your lines meet the diagonal band. Repeat all the way around the block (Fig. 1–4).

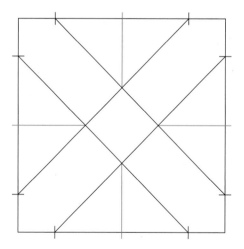

Fig. 1–3

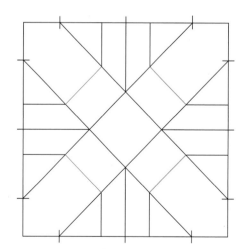

Fig. 1–5

- Draw a line from the center mark on the top to the center mark on the bottom, skipping over the center square. Repeat for the sides, again skipping over the center square (Fig. 1–3).

- With a ruler, join these new lines across the diagonal bands to complete the block. (Fig. 1–5)

You have just drawn your first Imagine Block! Drawing it this way is quick, though you could probably do it on a computer nearly as fast. This drawing method can be used to draft many kinds of blocks, from something as simple as a doodle, or from a sketch of an antique quilt block, or from some other source. You now have a basic tool for designing your own blocks and using them in fabulous quilts.

Fabric Considerations

For the simplest version of the Imagine Block, you only need three different fabrics. (Cotton is durable and easy to sew.) After you've chosen your main fabric and searched out accompanying fabrics from your collection or your favorite shop, it's time to decide which patches are to be cut from which fabrics.

As for the amount of fabric needed, if you are unsure how much to buy, ask the helpful people in your local quilt shop, or use this rule of thumb: If you need just a little bit, buy a quarter of a yard (or quarter of a meter). If you need a fair amount, buy a yard (one meter), and if you need a lot, buy three yards (three meters).

Should fabric be washed before being used in a quilt? Sometimes. Generally speaking, for a utility quilt, it's a good idea to wash and iron the fabrics before marking and cutting, but fabrics for wall hangings can be left unwashed. Some fabrics, however, reek of malodorous chemicals and need to be washed before you can be in the same room with them. If they still smell after two washes, throw them out, which is better than feeling sick in their presence.

Cutting Templates and Fabrics

Each of the six different patches in the block has a name: corner, rectangle (in some versions of the block the rectangle may in fact be a square), center square, triangle, pointer, and reverse pointer (Fig. 1–6).

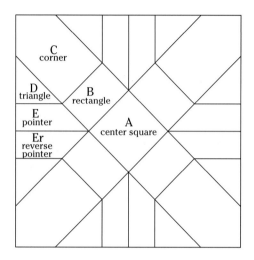

Fig. 1–6

Step by step

- On each patch in the cardboard square, write a brief description of your chosen fabric. For instance, write "paisley" for those patches to be cut from paisley, and write "dots" for those patches to be cut from dotted fabric.
- Carefully cut apart the six different cardboard templates. Reserve the rest in case you need to replace one that is worn out.
- It's a good idea to cut all the fabric patches to be made from one template at the same time. Start with the corner

template. Place it right side down on the wrong side of the fabric and draw around it with a sharp pencil. The pencil line will be your sewing line. As you trace the corner patches, allow for a ¼" (½ cm) seam allowance around each one. You don't have to measure the spacing, just cut the patches out at a distance from the pencil line that looks like a good ¼" allowance to you.

- Each IMAGINE BLOCK has four identical corner patches. Multiply the number of blocks in your quilt by 4 to determine how many corner patches to cut. For example, if you are planning a nine-block quilt, you will need to cut 36 corners (4 corners x 9 blocks). Set the corner patches aside, sorting them by fabric if you have used more than one.

- There are eight triangle patches in each block, so you can figure out how many you will need for the whole quilt, based on the number of blocks in your design. All triangles do not have to be cut from the same fabric. Again, draw around the template placed right side down on the wrong side of the fabric and cut as before. Sort triangle patches according to fabric.

- Repeat for the rectangle template, and put these patches in their own piles, sorted according to fabric.

- Next comes the pointer, and more so than with the previous patches, it is important that you put the right side of the template down on the wrong side of the fabric. The pointer patch is not symmetrical and can be turned the wrong way if you are not careful.

- Continue with the reverse pointer, again making sure to place the right side of the template down on the wrong side of the fabric. Sort the pieces according to fabric.

- There is only one center square in each block. Having cut them from the desired fabric and placed them in their own little pile, you are ready to sew the blocks.

Block Assembly

The blocks are pieced by sewing patches together to make units, then sewing the units together to make larger units, and so on to complete the blocks. The IMAGINE BLOCK lends itself very well to continuous (chain) piecing. You could almost sew an entire quilt with one seam.

Step by step

• Start by sewing a triangle to a pointer, right sides together, using the following method to match the seams: Stick a pin through one end of the seam line of the first patch. Then stick the pin through the end of the seam line of the second patch (Fig. 1–7). You will need to turn the second patch toward you slightly so you can see that the pin is coming through at the right place.

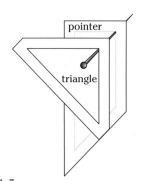

Fig. 1–7

• Pinch the fabrics together on the pin and, being careful not to let the fabrics shift, use a second pin to hold the patches together. Repeat for the other end of the seam line.

• Sew from raw edge to raw edge, following the drawn seam line, to complete the triangle/pointer unit (Fig. 1–8). Remove pins as you go. To chain sew the units, do not backstitch or cut the threads. Instead, sew a couple more stitches past the edge to form a little chain, insert the next triangle/pointer unit under the presser foot and sew them together (Fig. 1–9). Continue in this manner with all the units. After they have all been sewn, snip the chains to separate the units.

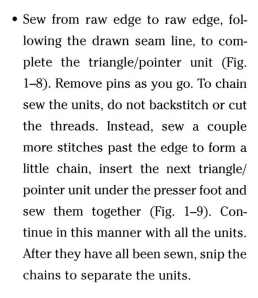

Fig. 1–8

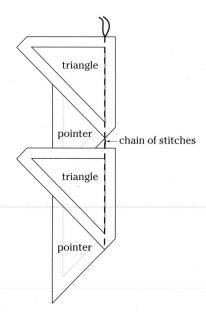

Fig. 1–9

One Block = Many Quilts *Agnete Kay*

- Pin the reverse pointers to triangles, right sides together, and chain sew all of these units as before. Snip the triangle/reverse pointer units apart.
- Pin and chain sew the two types of units together, aligning the pointer to the reverse pointer of each unit (Fig. 1–10). Snip the units apart.

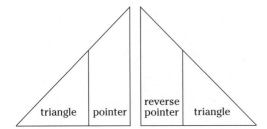

Fig. 1–10

- When all the units have been sewn and snipped apart, you are ready to press. Many quilters recommend pressing seam allowances toward the darker fabric, but consider pressing allowances open wherever possible. This technique distributes the bulk of the seam allowances and gives the quilt top a neater, flatter appearance.
- To sew a diagonal band, pin and sew the following patches in order: corner, rectangle, center square, rectangle, corner (Fig. 1–11). Complete one diagonal band for each block in your quilt design. Press the bands and set them aside.
- Sew the remaining corner patches to the last of rectangles to form the two partial diagonal bands (Fig. 1–12).

Diagonal band

Fig. 1–11

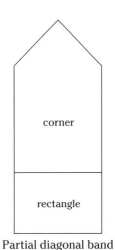

Partial diagonal band

Fig. 1–12

- Join a triangle/pointer unit to one side of a partial diagonal band and a triangle/reverse pointer unit to the other side of the band to form a large triangle (Fig. 1–13.) Pin a large triangle to each side of a whole diagonal band (Fig. 1–14). Carefully match the seams as you pin and then stitch to complete the block.

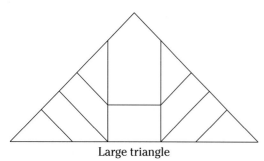

Large triangle

Fig. 1–13

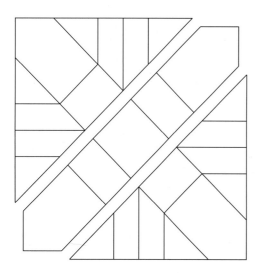

Fig. 1–14

Imagine the Possibilities

There are unlimited possibilities for varying the basic block. Several creations are shown on pages 19 and 20. Feel free to use these designs or, better yet, use the concepts presented to create your own unique blocks.

Sewing Tip: *Here is a good way to match seams as you sew: Pin units together with the pinheads sticking out beyond the edge to your right as the piece goes through the machine. When you are within one or two stitches of the seams or points you want to match, slow down and, with your right thumbnail, guide the pinhead gently past the needle. You will be sewing over the pin. One or two stitches past the seams, let go of the pin. This method keeps the fabrics from shifting while under the needle.*

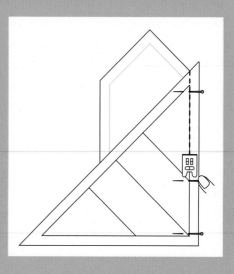

Narrow Diagonal Bands

Using the same 8½" square size, you can give the IMAGINE BLOCK a new look simply by varying the width of the Diagonal Bands. After drawing a square and marking the half-way points on all four sides, mark 1" (2.5 cm) in from the corners. Also, mark 1" on both sides of the half-way points. Follow the same basic instructions on page 13 for drawing the block (Fig. 1–15).

Wide Diagonal Bands

Again, begin with an 8½" square and mark the half-way points on each side. Your next marks will be 2" (5 cm) from the corners, and the next dividing mark 1⅛" (3 cm) from the half-way points. Based on these measurements, draw your new block (Fig. 1–16).

Double Diagonal Bands

This variation of the block is obtained by doubling the diagonal lines and connecting the subsequent lines across the new bands (Fig. 1–17). This new block I have named England's Rose.

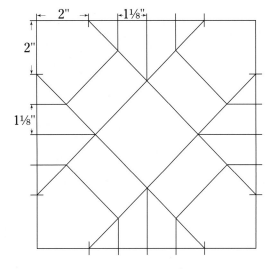

Fig. 1–16

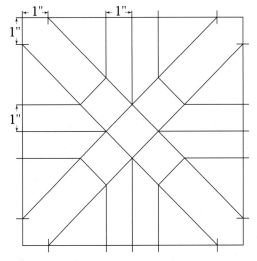

Fig. 1–15

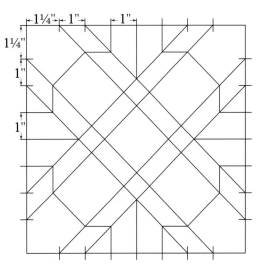

Fig. 1–17

Other Possibilities

You can easily change the block in other ways. Try slanting the lines for the diagonal bands (Fig. 1–18) or the pointers (Fig. 1–19), or turning the block into a rectangle (Fig. 1–20). See how simple it is to create a different look with the IMAGINE BLOCK!

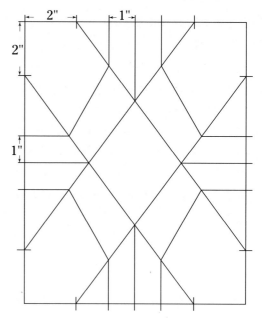

Fig. 1–20

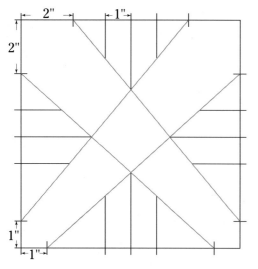

Fig. 1–18

Joining the Blocks

After you have pressed the completed blocks, it's time to put them all together. They can be joined in straight rows, all oriented the same direction, or for a different effect, you can turn every other block a quarter or half turn before it is joined to its neighbor. Lay the blocks out on a flat surface and study each possibility before you sew. Stitch the blocks together in rows, then sew the rows together, all the while matching points neatly.

Setting on Point

If the blocks are to be set on point, appearing as diamond shapes, you will need side triangles and corner triangles to square up the quilt top. For this type of quilt, the blocks are sewn together in diagonal rows, including the triangles (Fig. 1–21).

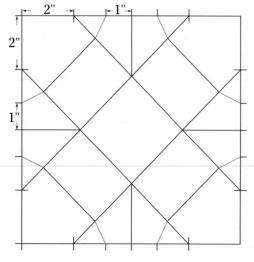

Fig. 1–19

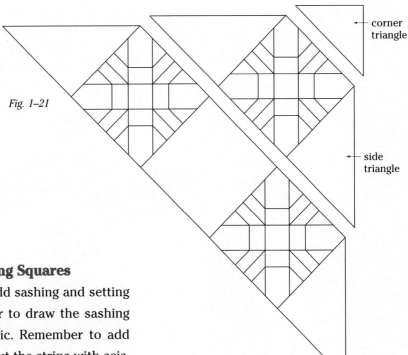

Fig. 1–21

corner triangle

side triangle

Sashing and Setting Squares

If you plan to add sashing and setting squares, use a ruler to draw the sashing strips on your fabric. Remember to add seam allowances. Cut the strips with scissors or a rotary cutter and cut the strips into sections, each the exact length of the block, including seam allowances. You will also need small setting squares in a contrasting fabric. The setting square dimensions should be equal to the sashing strip width with seam allowances.

Arrange the sashing strips, blocks, and setting squares on a flat surface so you can see the sewing sequence. Pin the blocks and sashing strips in rows as shown in Figure 1–22. Then sew the rows together.

Press and admire your quilt top! Pin it up on a wall and look at it for at least half an hour, better still a couple of days. If there is something you need to change, now is the time. Most likely you will love it, and it will gradually sink into your consciousness and become part of your world, like something that was always there.

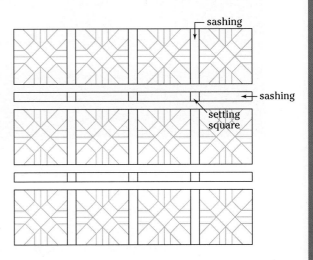

sashing

sashing

setting square

Fig. 1–22

AMISH I, 32" x 42", 1996, by the author. This quilt has six IMAGINE BLOCKS in a snowball-type setting with light circular areas formed by the colors used in the corners. All blocks are identical, with all patches cut from different fabrics. The quilting (stitched by hand, in red) is a "tartan" design, described in Chapter 4.

One Block = Many Quilts   *Agnete Kay*

CHAPTER 2

Imagine
the
Block
Patterns

Many years ago, I saw a picture of an antique quilt from the south of France. It consisted of a few relatively simple dark blocks in a center square, or medallion, surrounded by a very wide solid yellow border. It was so simple, yet so invigoratingly beautiful that it has inspired more than one quilt of mine.

Imagine
you are Amish

J ust as many composers can write a fugue in the style of Bach, but no one except Bach can actually write a Bach fugue, so all of us can imitate Amish quilts with solid colors and lots of black, but we can never get them exactly right. There always seems to be something missing, some sparkle gone. Many Amish-inspired quilts appear almost too neatly color-coordinated, whereas Amish quilters do not hesitate to put unexpected colors together.

We are used to thinking of light, medium, and dark in quilt patterns. What shocks me about many Amish quilts is that what I think of as dark is used as light. A very pleasant shock. It is as if the quilter is telling me there is light even in the dark.

AMISH II has four IMAGINE BLOCKS with wide diagonal bands. The blocks are set on point, with a solid-black background, consisting of a plain block in the middle, four half-square triangles in the corners, and four quarter-square triangles on the sides.

Because the corner patches are black, when the block is joined with a black background, it looks rather like one seen in Amish quilts called Hole in the Barn Door, though of course, it isn't like it at all.

The block setting is framed by an olive green border. It is usually a "no-no" to introduce a color in the border that has not been used in the center of the quilt, but Amish quiltmakers do it all the time.

The width of the black border was determined by how much black fabric I had left – a perfectly good reason, I might add. The quilt was machine-quilted in the ditch and wherever I thought a line of quilting was needed. The center black square was quilted with tartan-like lines.

AMISH II, 38½" x 38½", 1997, by the author.

Imagine
you are Amish

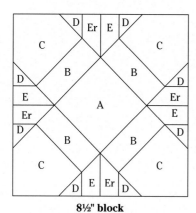

8½" block

For templates, cut on dashed line (pg. 14).
For rotary cutting, use solid line.
r = reverse.

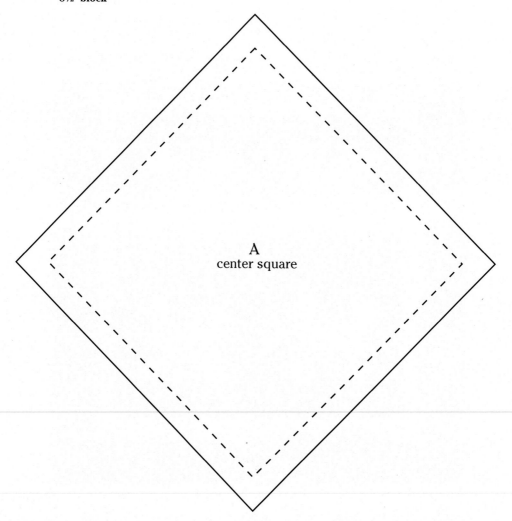

A
center square

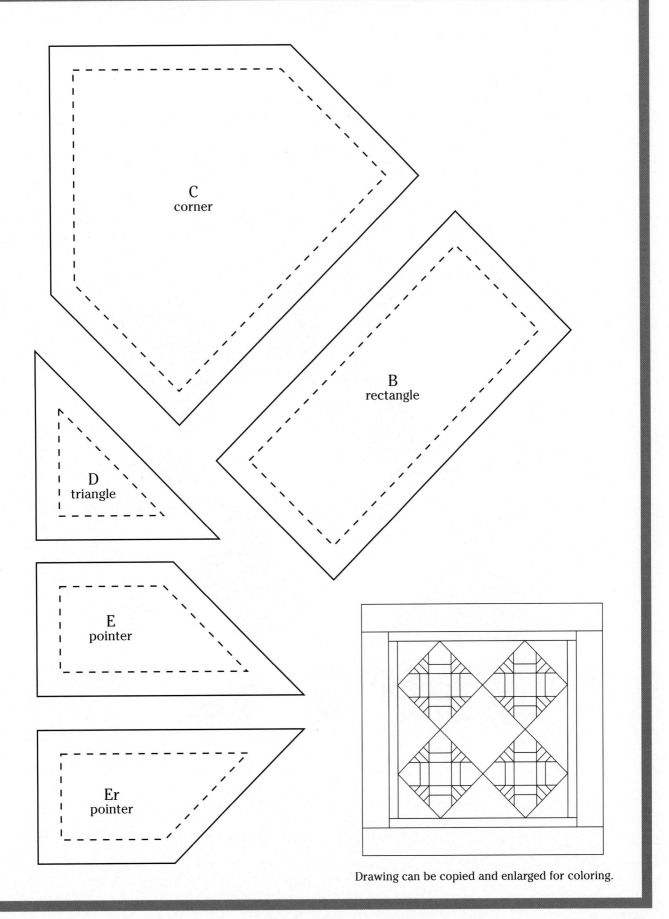

C
corner

B
rectangle

D
triangle

E
pointer

Er
pointer

Drawing can be copied and enlarged for coloring.

Imagine

Op-Art is back in fashion

Remember Op-Art? That 1960s style was characterized by black and white squares that weren't always square, and they appeared to grow, shrink, and undulate.

One Block = Many Quilts   *Agnete Kay*

Start with your cardboard square, but instead of drawing the two diagonal bands as parallel lines, make them wider on one end and narrower on the other. The triangles, pointers, and corners will have odd shapes, and you can fiddle with the diagonal lines until the shapes please you.

When you join rows of blocks together, match the narrow ends of the diagonal bands with the narrow ends of the adjacent blocks, and wide ends with wide ends, so that the seams meet.

The center of the blocks in the quilt called Op-Art was cut from a reddish print. All the other patches in the block alternate, light against dark, dark against light. To achieve this effect in your own IMAGINE quilt, start with any patch on your cardboard template. Write on it either "dark" or "light," and write on each neighboring patch the opposite value. Continue alternating light and dark, in checkerboard fashion, until all the template pieces have been marked.

OP-ART, 51" x 51", 1996, by the author.

Imagine

Op-Art is back in fashion

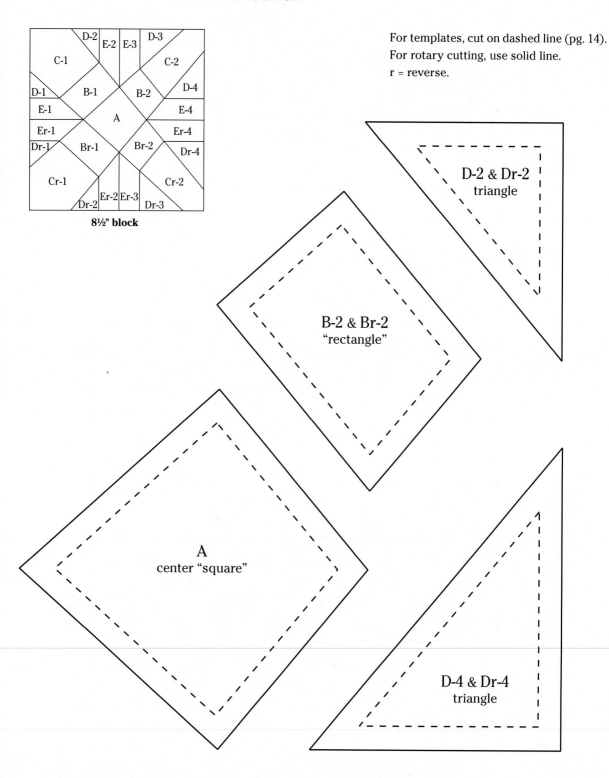

8½" block

For templates, cut on dashed line (pg. 14).
For rotary cutting, use solid line.
r = reverse.

D-2 & Dr-2 triangle

B-2 & Br-2 "rectangle"

A center "square"

D-4 & Dr-4 triangle

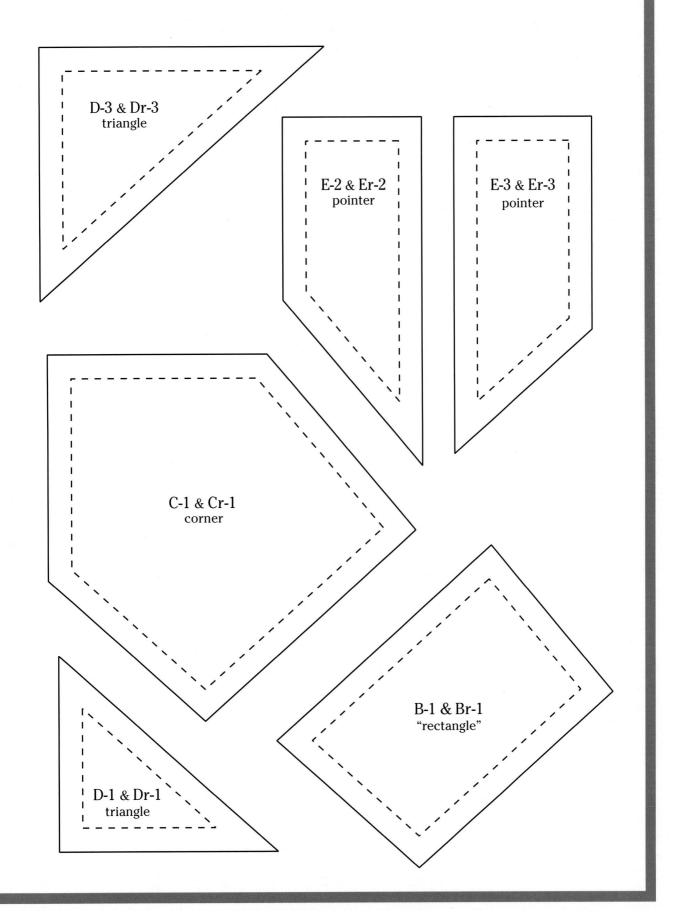

D-3 & Dr-3
triangle

E-2 & Er-2
pointer

E-3 & Er-3
pointer

C-1 & Cr-1
corner

B-1 & Br-1
"rectangle"

D-1 & Dr-1
triangle

Imagine
Op-Art is back in fashion

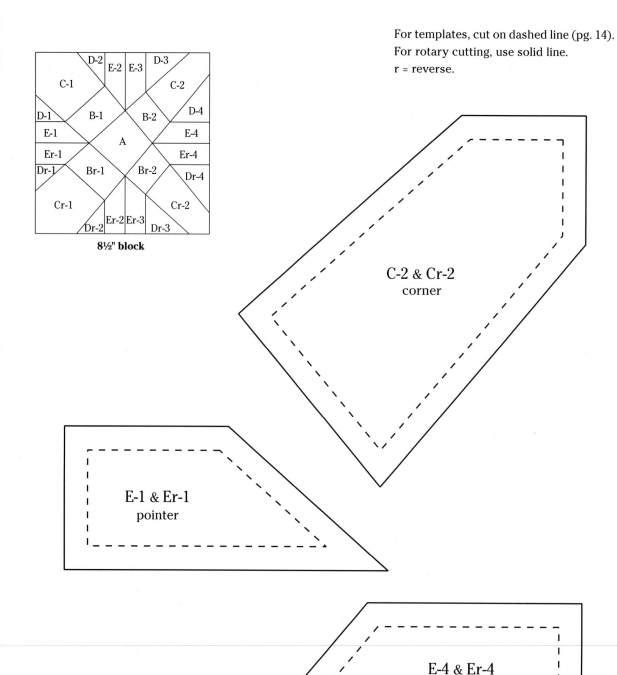

For templates, cut on dashed line (pg. 14).
For rotary cutting, use solid line.
r = reverse.

8½" block

C-2 & Cr-2
corner

E-1 & Er-1
pointer

E-4 & Er-4
pointer

Drawing can be copied and enlarged for coloring.

Imagine
revisiting
No. 11 Tulip Avenue

As the result of a quilt challenge containing a tulip print, it was inevitable that I would make a quilt in remembrance of our few years in Denmark. There we lived in a white brick bungalow at No. 11 Tulip Avenue. Neighboring streets were also named for flowers, like iris and daisy, hence my choice of added fabrics.

One Block = Many Quilts   *Agnete Kay*

This block was drawn just like the other IMAGINE BLOCKS, except the lines on either side of the center are slightly angled. Notice the flowers in the center.

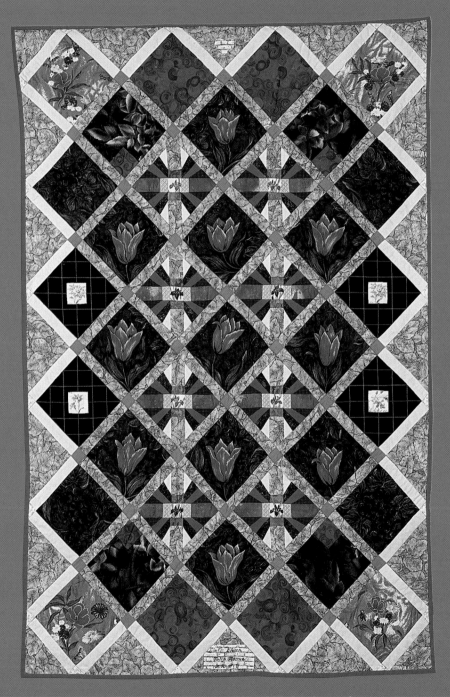

TULIP AVENUE, 41" x 61", 1997, by the author.

Imagine
revisiting
No. 11 Tulip Avenue

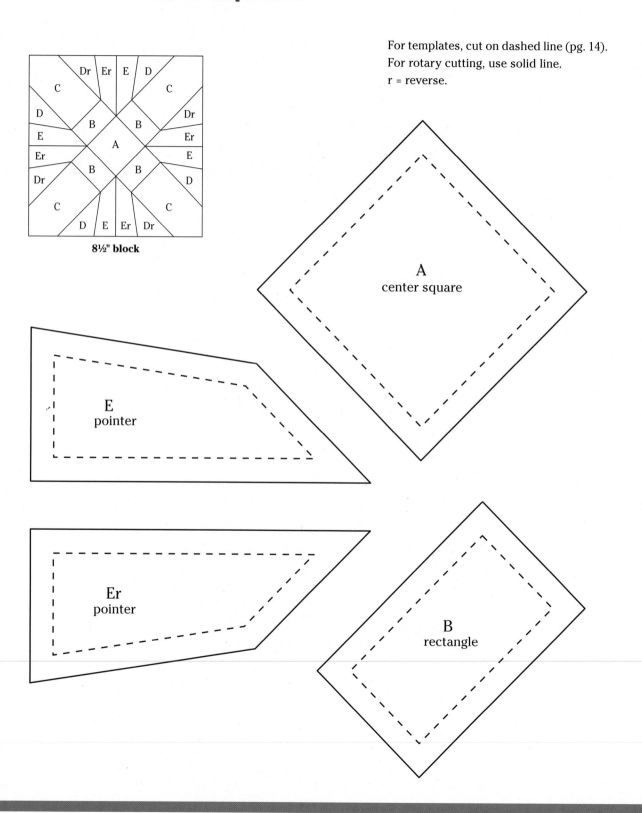

8½" block

For templates, cut on dashed line (pg. 14).
For rotary cutting, use solid line.
r = reverse.

A
center square

E
pointer

Er
pointer

B
rectangle

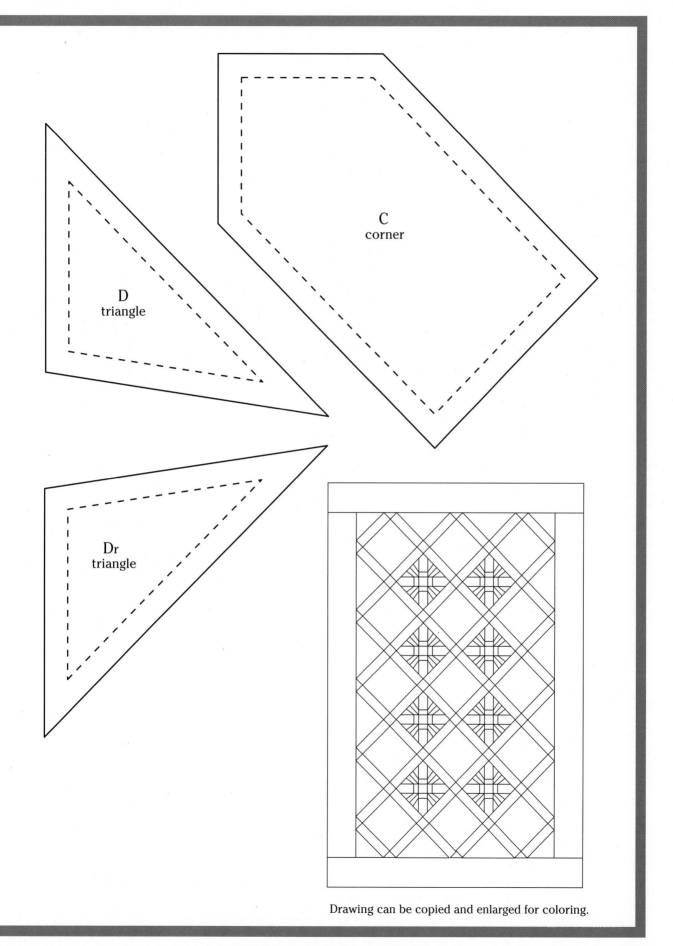

D
triangle

C
corner

Dr
triangle

Drawing can be copied and enlarged for coloring.

Imagine
you have a cover quilt

Generally, to make it to the cover of a magazine, a quilt has to be either very old or a tour-de-force, or both. Now, tour-de-force quilts are not for everyone. If I have worked six months on a quilt, there is invariably someone who has worked six years. I have too many ideas for one lifetime as it is, so I would not want to spend that much time on one quilt. But I can imagine having a cover quilt.

For my "cover" quilt, I wanted to see if the IMAGINE BLOCKS could look like baskets if they were assembled with light and dark fabrics in the right places. Each block in Yukon Christmas Baskets is divided into four quarters, and each quarter is part of a different basket. The baskets emerge when the blocks are set together.

The block for this quilt is made with wide diagonal bands. Two different alternating blocks are needed to make the baskets stand out. You can think of them as winter and summer blocks. There should be an even number of blocks per row.

To finish the quilt top, a "border" of half-blocks was added, which completes all the baskets. To make this outer edge of half-baskets appear more border-like, the same color scheme was used, but in lighter fabrics.

Before you start tracing and cutting, it's a good idea to make a color reference for piecing. You can draw the whole quilt top and write the fabric type on each patch, or better still, color the patches.

To add the heart and bow embellishments, after the blocks have been sewn together, cut a small paper heart shape, about 2" (5 cm) high. Using the paper template, trace and cut a heart for each basket. Pin the hearts in place. At the top of each one, insert the two ends of a short piece of gold cord or ribbon to form a loop.

To avoid pulling the hearts out of shape while you sew them, for each heart place a sheet of paper under the quilt top to act as a stabilizer. Machine stitch around the hearts with satin or zigzag stitches, catching the ends of the loops in the stitches. The paper will tear off easily afterward.

A 25-basket quilt can be used as a child's Christmas calendar with a small present attached to each gold loop for the first 24 days of December. To the one extra basket, attach a Christmas ornament, such as a wreath, angel, or bow.

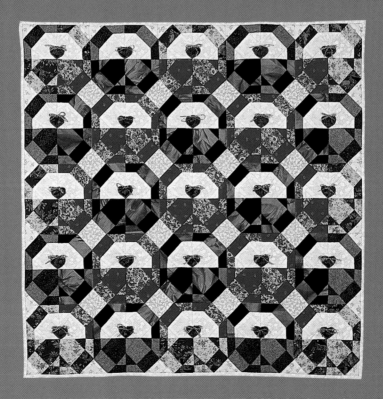

YUKON CHRISTMAS BASKETS, 47" x 47", 1994, by the author.

Imagine
you have
a cover quilt

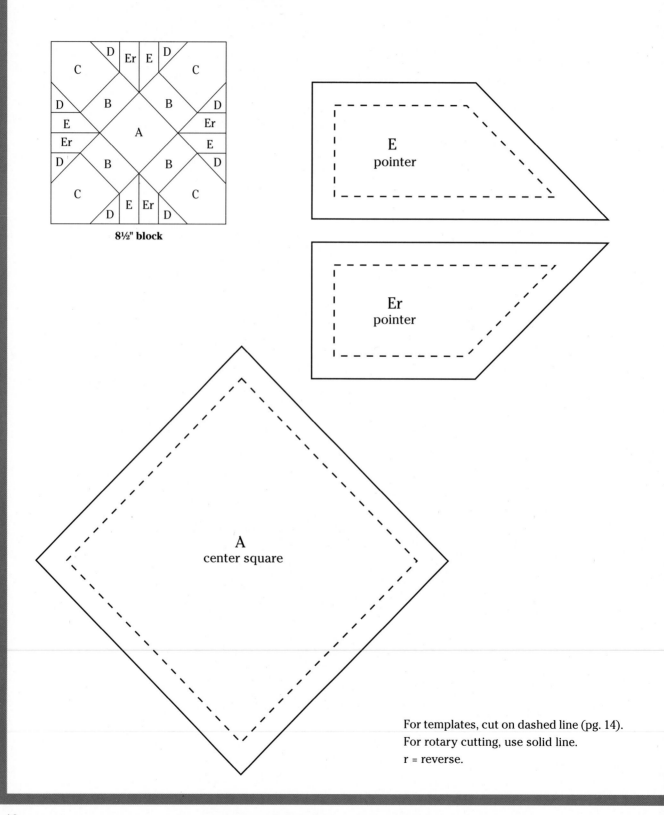

8½" block

E
pointer

Er
pointer

A
center square

For templates, cut on dashed line (pg. 14).
For rotary cutting, use solid line.
r = reverse.

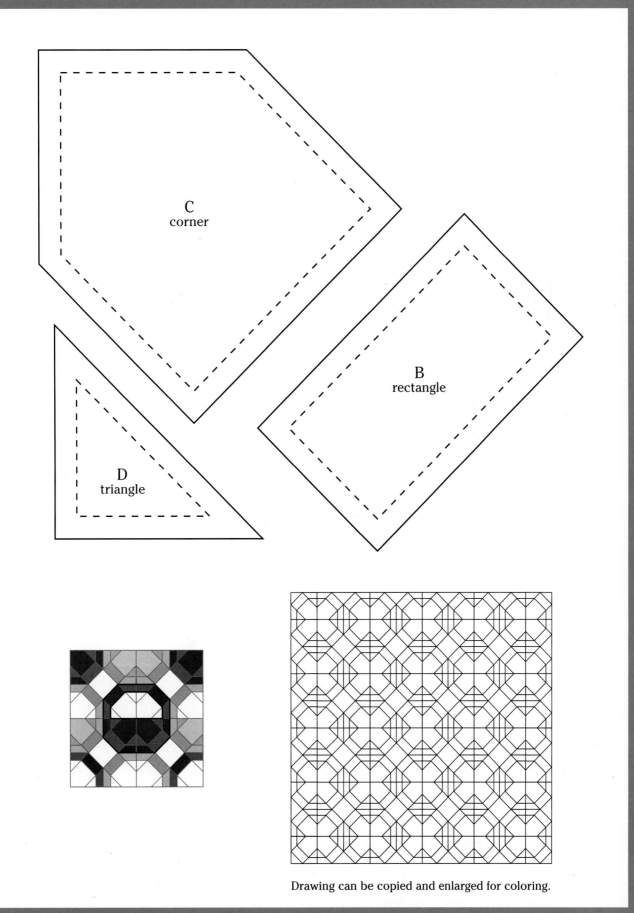

C
corner

B
rectangle

D
triangle

Drawing can be copied and enlarged for coloring.

Imagine
you are in
Serendip

A traditional Korean white silk dress I once saw had square panels appliquéd along the lower edge of the skirt. These brightly colored squares,
which were set on point, may have been patchwork, and with a little
adaptation, this IMAGINE BLOCK is not unlike that design.

I placed the blocks on point on a white and pale-blue length of cotton, thinking I would achieve a Korean-looking wall hanging. Instead, it turned out rather
like a Ukrainian Easter towel. In Serendip, you serendipitously get the delightfully
unexpected. A table runner with a Korean motif turned out to be perfect for dis-
playing a bowl filled with Ukrainian Easter eggs. Imagine!

Four blocks in gold, white, and red, like the Korean originals, (framed in a red border cut from 2" [5 cm] wide strips,) are appliquéd to a background. The blocks, made in your personal color scheme, could also be appliquéd to a jacket or vest. A table runner with one block at each end is also a possibility.

Appliqué the blocks to a background by turning under the allowance on all four sides of the red border that frames the block. Press the turn-under allowance. Pin the blocks in place on the background fabric and machine stitch with red thread. Other appropriate choices would include blind, blanket, and zigzag stitches.

SERENDIPITY, 36" x 45", 1995, by the author.

Imagine
you are in
Serendip

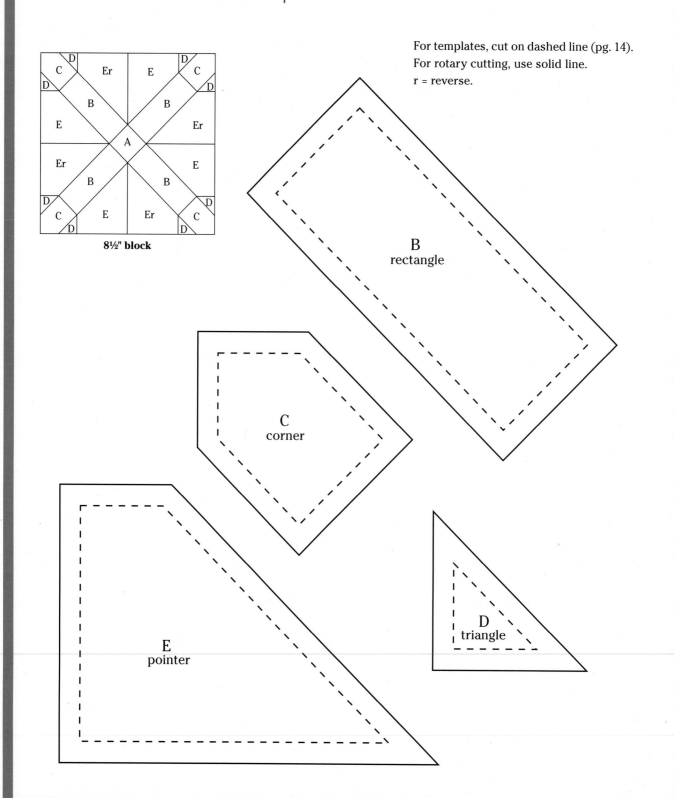

8½" block

For templates, cut on dashed line (pg. 14).
For rotary cutting, use solid line.
r = reverse.

B
rectangle

C
corner

E
pointer

D
triangle

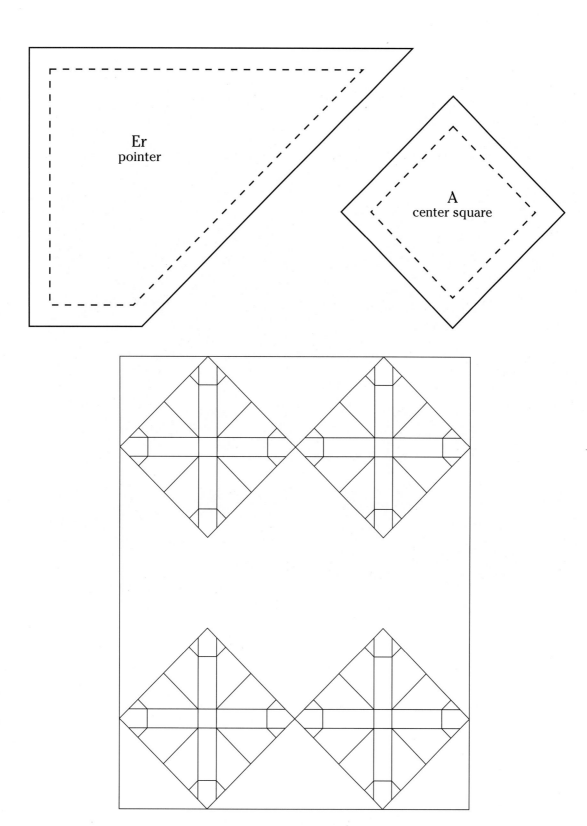

Er
pointer

A
center square

Drawing can be copied and enlarged for coloring.
Blocks are appliquéd to background.

ROSE WINDOW, 30" x 30", 1996, by the author. For a challenge, we were to make a quilt in medieval style and use fabrics designed by Barbara Chainey. It is sometimes said that contest rules and challenges restrict the creative mind. To me, the opposite is true. I find it very inspiring to have to make something pretty with limited means. See if you can find the IMAGINE BLOCK in this quilt. There are eight of them.

CHAPTER 3

Imagine
the Quilt Patterns

When I began sewing lessons in grade 2 in Denmark, Miss Jespersen told everyone to bring a sewing bag to keep our stuff in. I imagined my stepmother would buy a neat piece of cotton and sew me a bag, but instead she dug out of her trunk an old black silken bag with drawstring and tassels. It had floral embroidery in red and green, a typical piece of work from the Victorian era made by some long-departed relative. She said it was the perfect sewing bag. I absolutely hated it. It was ugly, and worse than that, unfashionable. As soon as I could get away with it, I threw it out. How different I feel now!

Imagine
you are in
Edwardian Wales

*I*magine you are in Wales in the first decade of this century. Maybe you are a proud housewife in a miner's cottage. The coal fire is burning cheerfully in the giant kitchen fireplace, and you finally have a moment, hot tea at the ready, to begin a scrap quilt made from chintzes and dress fabric remnants. It will be a medallion quilt, with a few blocks in the center, surrounded by two or more simple borders made from plain squares.

There are just four identical IMAGINE BLOCKS in this medallion quilt. You might use mainly brown, blue, and rusty red prints. Fabrics that look a little old-fashioned would be good. Many other colors can be used, naturally, but there seems to have been a prevalence of those three colors in that era.

WELSH MEDALLION, 29" x 29", 1995, by the author.

WELSH MEDALLION
Quilt 28" x 28"
4 Blocks 7" x 7"

Fabric Requirements
(based on 42"-wide fabric)

Fabrics	Yards	Pieces
Floral 1	⅛	4 C
Floral 2	¼	8 F
Floral 3	¼	8 F
Green	⅛	8 D
Gold	⅛	8 D
Red 1	⅛	4 B
Red 2	⅜	4 E, 4 Er
Blue 1	⅛	4 E, 4 Er
Blue 2	⅛	4 B
Navy 1	⅛	8 B
Navy 2	⅜	8 D, 8 F
Cream	⅛	4 E, 4 Er
*Stripe	⅝	8 C, 16 F
Tan	⅛	4 A
Brown	¼	4 E, 4 Er, 4 F
Plaid	⅛	4 C
Black	¼	8 D, 4 F
**Binding		2 strips 1¾" x 32"
		2 strips 1¾" x 30"
Backing	1	1 panel 32" x 32"
Batting		32" x 32"

*A see-through plastic template would be useful for controlling the placement of the stripes in the patches. If you can't find a suitable striped fabric for your quilt, you can make your own by sewing strips of various widths together.

**Binding yardage is based on the method described on page 106.

Assembly
Blocks
- Cut binding strips across the width of the bright red fabric and set aside.
- Cut all the patches as listed under Fabric Requirements. You may want to label the fabrics with the designations used in the Fabric Requirements table to help you keep track of them. Alternatively, you can make a rough, small drawing of the quilt and tape swatches on the drawing. This can even be done in the store as you buy your fabrics. Template patterns are provided for this quilt on pages 53–54.
- Because color placement is important for producing this design, you may want to arrange all your patches on a flat surface before you begin sewing the blocks. Following the Quilt Assembly diagram for color and position, use

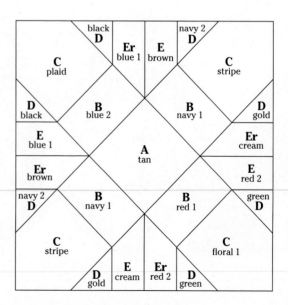

Block Piecing

continuous piecing, described on page 16, to sew the four blocks.

- Join the blocks together in two rows of two, paying attention to how the blocks are turned to achieve the design. Then sew the rows together.

Borders

- Following the Quilt Assembly diagram for color placement, construct one strip of the inner border by alternating two floral-2 patches (F's) with two floral-3 F's. Make four of these strips.

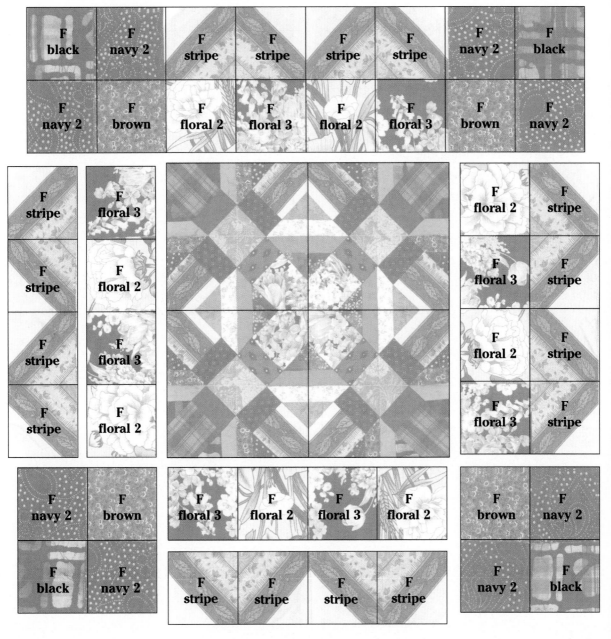

Quilt Assembly

Making sure the strips are positioned correctly, sew strips to two opposite sides of the quilt. Sew a brown F to each end of the remaining border strips. Sew these strips to the other sides of the quilt. Use the same construction method to add the outer border to the quilt, paying attention to the rotation of the striped patches.

Quilting and Finishing

• General instructions for layering, quilting, and binding begin on page 104. A simple grid of in-the-ditch quilting runs across the quilt horizontally and vertically, outlining the plain squares and dividing the blocks into quarters, as shown in the Quilting Pattern 1 diagram. You could also quilt along the edges of the stripes and diagonally across the center of the quilt, following the diagonal bands as in Quilting Pattern 2.

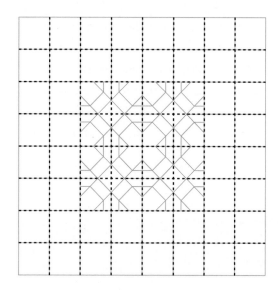

Quilting Pattern 1

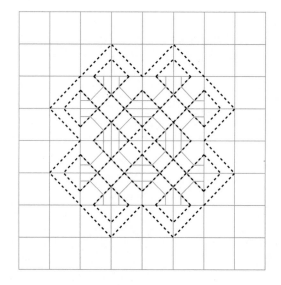

Quilting Pattern 2

One Block = Many Quilts   *Agnete Kay*

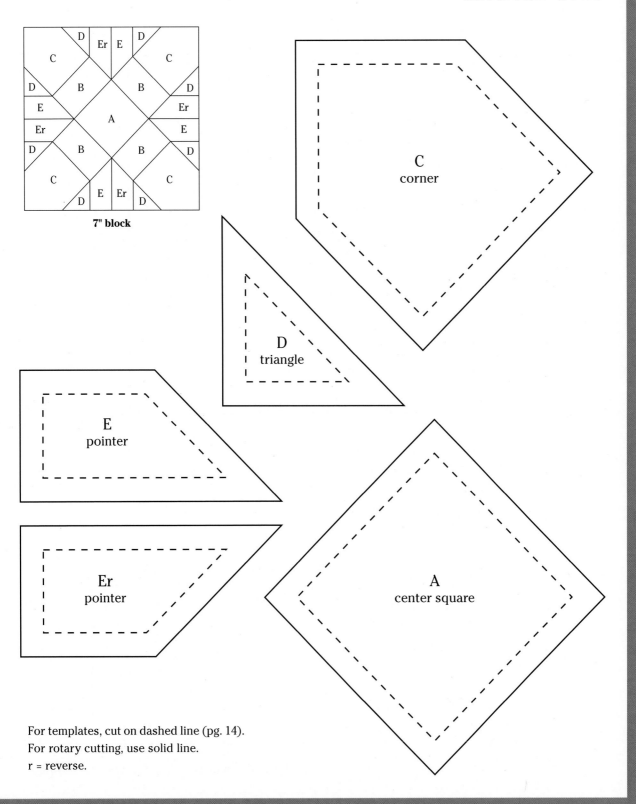

7" block

C
corner

D
triangle

E
pointer

Er
pointer

A
center square

For templates, cut on dashed line (pg. 14).
For rotary cutting, use solid line.
r = reverse.

Imagine
you are in
Edwardian Wales

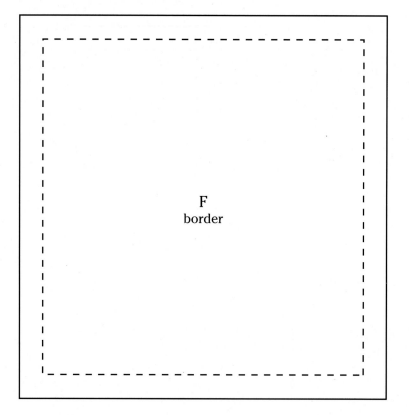

F
border

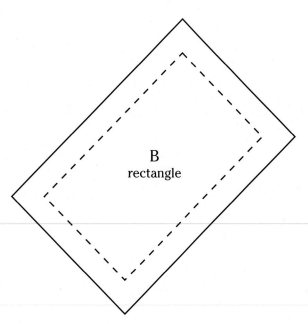

B
rectangle

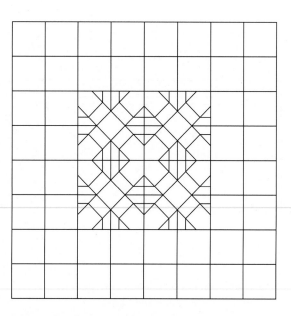

Drawing can be copied and enlarged for coloring.

Imagine

you are in Mexico

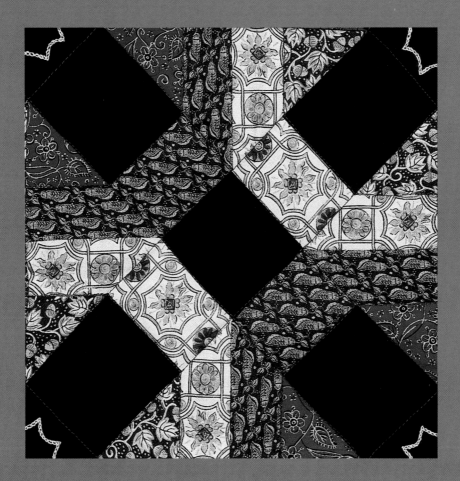

O ne day in 1971, while we were living in Manchester, England, I passed a fabric shop and looked in. There I saw the most gorgeous printed cotton I had ever seen. I can still see it in my mind's eye. It was blue and black, purple, pink and white, with large lovely flowers, and it was made by Rose & Hubble. That was probably the first time I had encountered a piece of fabric I just had to have, it was so beautiful. In those days, I hardly knew anything about patchwork, so all I could think of was making a dress, which in the end was just so-so. Who would have guessed that, 25 years later, my quilt Mexico would be a finalist in a quilt challenge issued by none other than Rose & Hubble? Life is full of surprises.

In this quilt, four golden fabrics call forth the ancient golden age of Mexico. The black patches create a woven effect, and a matching border was constructed by continuing some lines from the block. The Rose & Hubble challenge was called "Just Add Black." This quilt was a finalist, and it traveled with a show for two years in the United Kingdom and the United States.

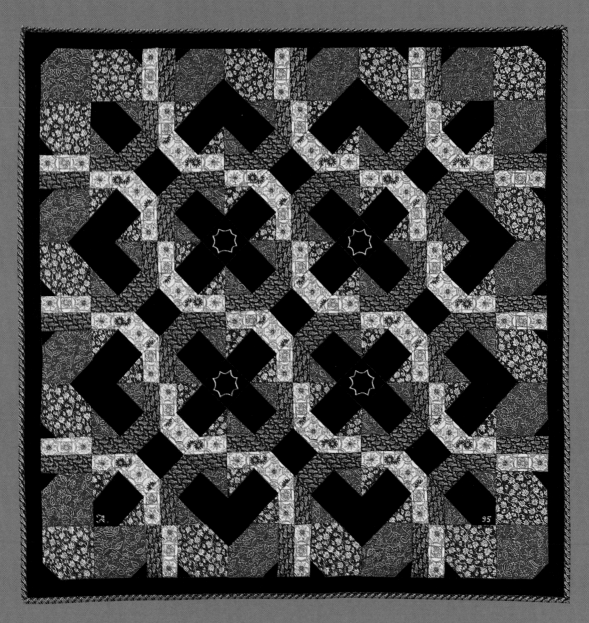

MEXICO, 34½" x 34½", 1995, by the author.

One Block = Many Quilts *Agnete Kay*

MEXICO
Quilt 34½" x 34½"
9 Blocks 8½" x 8½"

Fabric Requirements
(based on 42"-wide fabric)

Fabrics	Yards	Pieces
Red Print	½	36 D, 8 F, 6 H
Burgundy Print	½	36 D, 8 F, 6 H
White Print	½	18 B, 18 E, 18 Er, 12 I
Black	¾	9 A, 36 C, 28 G, 16 J
Border		2 strips 1½" x 36½"
		2 strips 1½" x 34½"
Green Print	¾	18 B, 18 E, 18 Er, 12 I
*Binding		2 strips 1¾" x 38½"
		2 strips 1¾" x 36½"
Backing	1⅛	1 panel 38½" x 38½"
Batting		38½" x 38½"

*Binding yardage is based on the method described beginning on page 106.

Assembly
Blocks

- Cut border and binding strips across the width of the fabrics and set aside.
- Cut all the patches as listed under Fabric Requirements. Template patterns for this quilt are provided on pages 60–62.
- Refer to the Block Assembly diagram and use continuous piecing, described on page 16, to make the nine blocks.
- Join the blocks together in three rows of three, and sew the rows together to complete the center of the quilt.

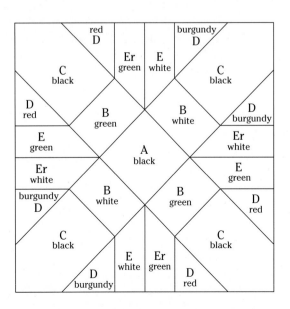

Block Assembly

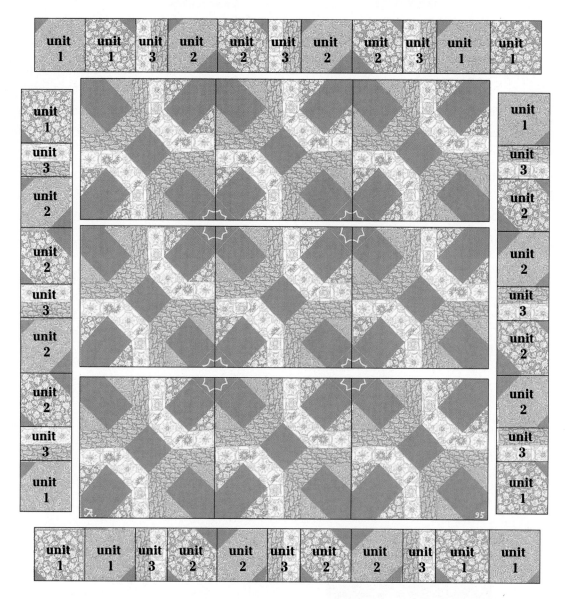

Quilt Assembly

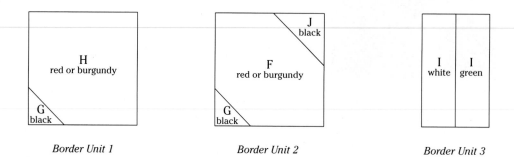

Border Unit 1

Border Unit 2

Border Unit 3

One Block = Many Quilts   *Agnete Kay*

Borders

- Following the Quilt Assembly diagram for color placement, make six red Unit 1's, six burgundy Unit 1's, eight red Unit 2's, eight burgundy Unit 2's, and 12 Unit 3's.
- Sew the units together in strips, as shown in the Quilt Assembly diagram, and sew the strips to the quilt top.

Quilting and Finishing

- The general instructions for layering, quilting, and binding your quilt can be found beginning on page 104. Mexico is quilted in the ditch along the edges of the diagonal bands and vertically and horizontally along the outside edges of the pointers (see the Quilting Pattern diagram below.)

Quilting Pattern

Imagine
you are in
Mexico

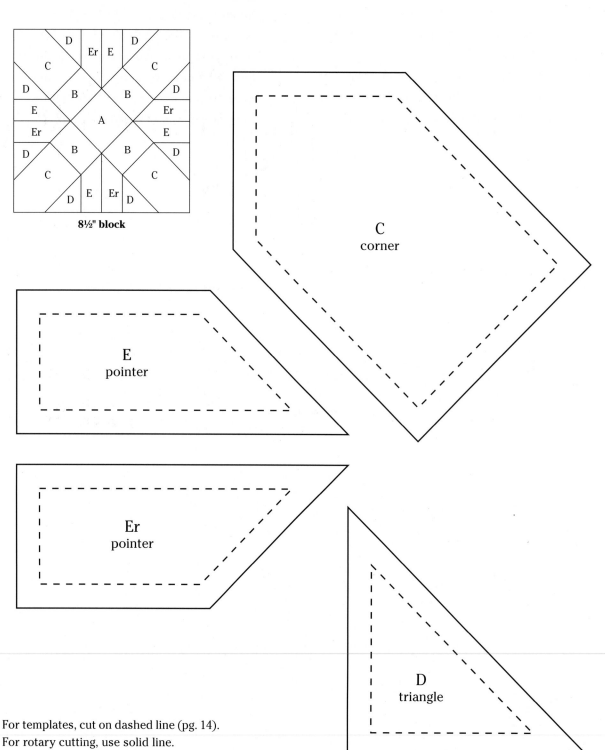

8½" block

C
corner

E
pointer

Er
pointer

D
triangle

For templates, cut on dashed line (pg. 14).
For rotary cutting, use solid line.
r = reverse.

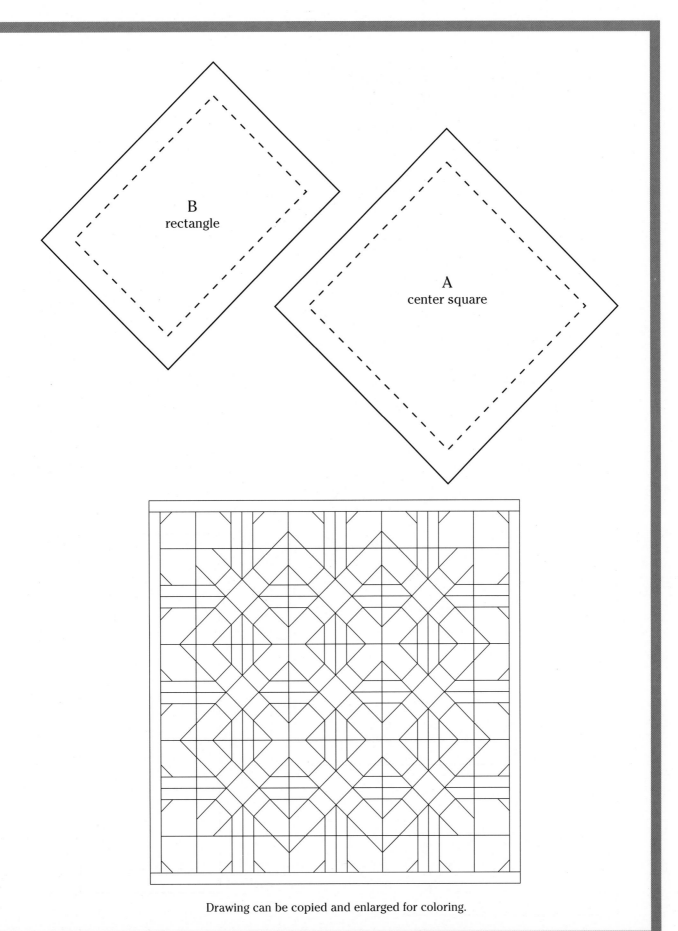

B
rectangle

A
center square

Drawing can be copied and enlarged for coloring.

Imagine
you are in
Mexico

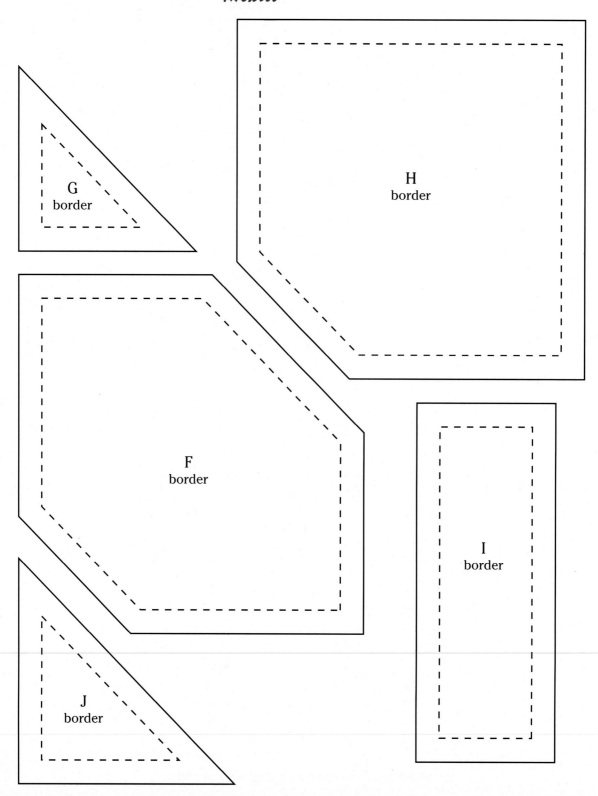

G
border

H
border

F
border

I
border

J
border

One Block = Many Quilts *Agnete Kay*

Imagine
a gingham rhapsody

As for the word "gingham," the dark, light, and medium blocks in the quilt *Rhapsodic Gingham Pastiche* are set to look like a gingham weave. As for "rhapsodic," well, it is strange that not more quilts are called rhapsodies since the literal meaning of the word is something woven or stitched together.

Notice that Rhapsodic Gingham Pastiche contains 25 blocks with identical construction, but three different color schemes. There are 4 light, 12 medium, and 9 dark blocks with 3 fabrics in each block. You can use prints or solids or a combination of the two. Sort your fabrics into light, medium, and dark piles. Then sort each of those piles into light, medium, and dark to create a total of nine piles.

RHAPSODIC GINGHAM PASTICHE, 50½" x 50½", 1996, by the author.

One Block = Many Quilts *Agnete Kay*

RHAPSODIC GINGHAM PASTICHE

Quilt 50½" x 50½"
25 Blocks 9½" x 9½"

Fabric Requirements
(based on 42"-wide fabric)

Fabrics	Yards	Pieces
LIGHT BLOCKS		
White	⅜	8 B, 16 D, 8 E
		8 Er
Cream 1	¼	4 A, 16 C
Cream 2	⅜	8 B, 16 D, 8 E
		8 Er,
Border		4 G, 4 Gr
MEDIUM BLOCKS		
Black 1	⅝	24 B, 48 D, 24 E
		24 Er
Lavender 1	¾	12 A, 48 C
Lavender 2	¾	24 B, 48 D, 24 E
		24 Er
DARK BLOCKS		
Blue	⅝	18 B, 36 D, 18 E
		18 Er
Black 2	⅝	9 A, 36 C
Black 3	⅞	18 B, 36 D, 18 E
		18 Er
Border		4 F, 8 H
		4 strips 1¾" x 42"
Black solid	½	
*Binding (pieced)		2 strips 1¾" x 56"
		2 strips 1¾" x 53"
Backing	¼	2 panels
		28" x 54½"
Batting		54½" x 54½"

*Binding yardage is based on the method described on page 106.

Assembly

Blocks

- Cut border strips across the width of the fabric and set aside.
- Cut all the rest of the pieces listed under Fabric Requirements. Template patterns for this quilt are provided on pages 68–69.
- Refer to the Block Assembly diagrams for the color and position of the patches and use continuous piecing, described on page 16, to sew the 4 light, 12 medium, and 9 dark blocks.
- Sew the blocks together in rows, as shown in the Quilt Assembly diagram. Then sew the rows together.

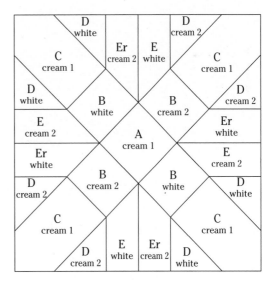

Light Block

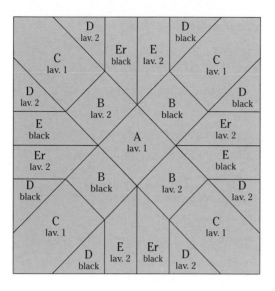

Medium Block

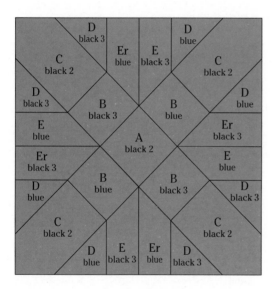

Dark Block

Border

- Border strips are slightly longer than needed to allow room for adjustments. To determine how long the border strips should actually be, measure your quilt top on all four sides. Add the four measurements together and divide by 4 to find the average border length. Add ½" for seam allowances to the average length. Trim the four border strips to this length.

- Refer to the Border Unit diagrams and make 4 of each one. Being careful to orient the units properly, sew a Border Unit 1 to one side of each border strip and a Border Unit 2 to the other side. Sew border strips to two opposite sides of the quilt. Sew an F patch to each end of the remaining border strips and sew the strips to the top and bottom of the quilt to complete the quilt top.

Quilting and Finishing

- General instructions for layering, quilting, and binding begin on page 104. Quilting stitches run down the center of all the diagonal bands. Other diagonal in-the-ditch quilting lines wind their way across the quilt, following the outside edges of the pointers and crossing the diagonal bands between the B and C patches, as shown in the Quilting Pattern diagram.

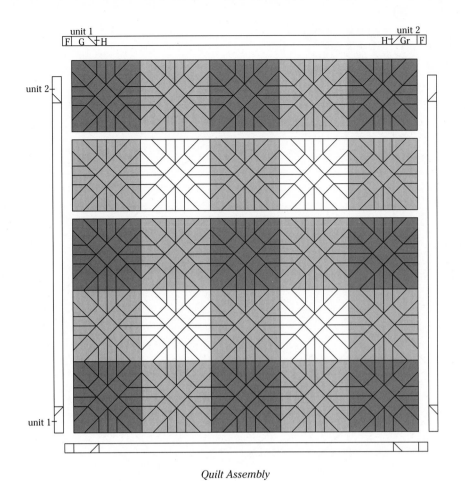

unit 1
F G H

unit 2
H Gr F

unit 2

unit 1

Quilt Assembly

F
black 3

G
cream 1

black 3
H

Border Unit 1

black 3
H

Gr
cream 1

F
black 3

Border Unit 2

Quilting Pattern

Imagine
a gingham rhapsody

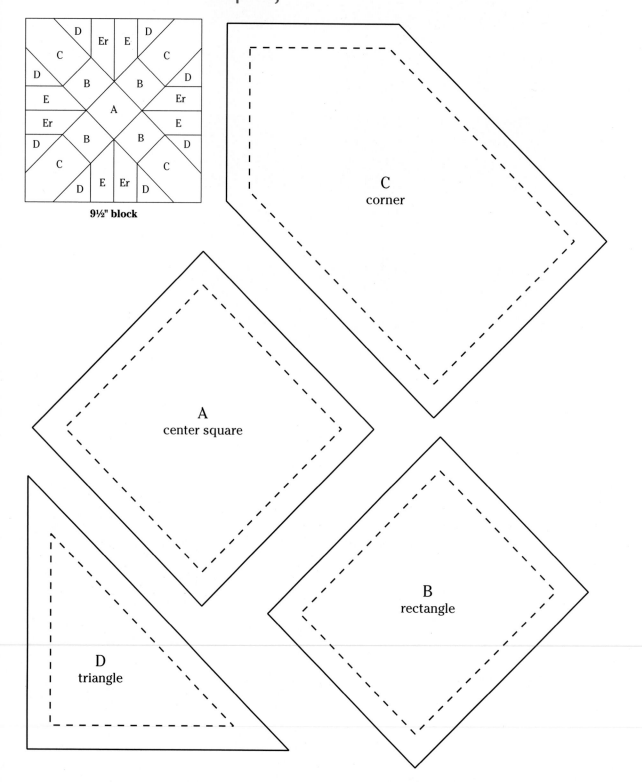

9½" block

C
corner

A
center square

B
rectangle

D
triangle

One Block = Many Quilts   *Agnete Kay*

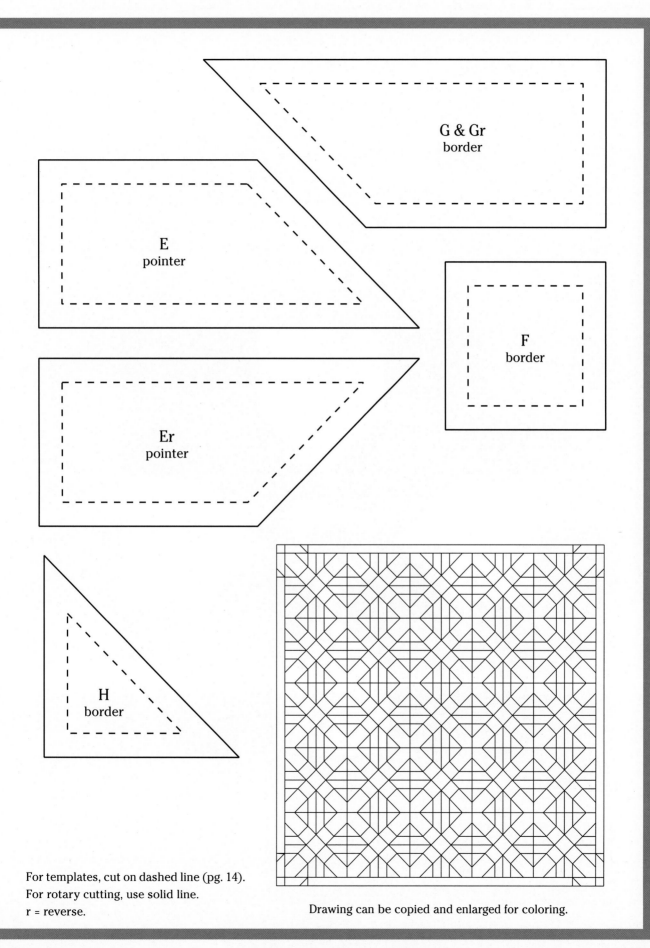

G & Gr
border

E
pointer

F
border

Er
pointer

H
border

For templates, cut on dashed line (pg. 14).
For rotary cutting, use solid line.
r = reverse.

Drawing can be copied and enlarged for coloring.

Imagine
you were a carpet weaver in a previous life

The colors and designs of Oriental carpets never cease to fascinate me. I made this miniature quilt in the style of an antique carpet, with some dark blocks and some light, all set on point.

To make the alternating dark and light blocks appear interlocked, the pointers in the dark blocks are made from fabrics in the light blocks. When making very small blocks, cut extra-wide allowances and trim them to ⅛" after the patches have been joined.

SMALL CARPET, 15½" x 21", 1996, by the author.

SMALL CARPET

Quilt 15½" x 21"

8 Blocks 3¾" x 3¾"

Fabric Requirements
(based on 42"-wide fabric)

Fabrics	Yards	Pieces
White Print	⅛	48 E
Light Floral 1	⅛	24 Er, 4 N
Light Floral 2	¼	14 C, 24 Er, 6 F, 6 Fr
Cream Print	½	14 B, 12 G, 4 I, 4 Ir
*Binding		2 strips 1½" x 23"
		2 strips 1½" x 21"
Tan Print	¼	40 D, 4 M
Red	¼	2 A, 6 H, 40 L
Dark Floral	¼	24 C
**Border 1		2 strips 1¼" x 18"
		2 strips 1¼ x 13"
Dark Print	¼	48 D, 24 B, 4 J
**Border 3		2 strips 1¼" x 22"
		2 strips 1¼" x 17"
Blue Floral	¼	6 A, 8D, 20 K
Backing	⅝	1 panel 20" x 25"
Batting		20" x 25"

*Binding yardage is based on the method described on page 106.

**Border 2 is pieced from L and K patches (see Border Assembly diagram, page 74).

Assembly

Blocks

- Cut binding and border strips across the width of the appropriate fabrics and set aside.

- Cut all the patches as listed under Fabric Requirements. Template patterns for this quilt are provided on page 75–76.

- Accurate sizing of blocks is important for fitting a pieced border. Refer to the Block Assembly diagram and make a sample block from scraps. Measure the block to make sure it is 4¼" x 4¼", including seam allowances. If it is not, adjust the allowance width and make another sample block. When you have determined the correct allowance width to produce a 4¼" block, make the two light blocks and six dark blocks, using continuous piecing, described on page 16.

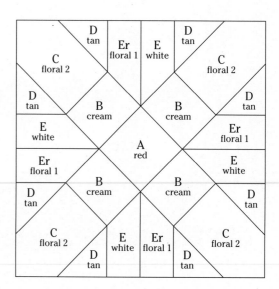

Light Block

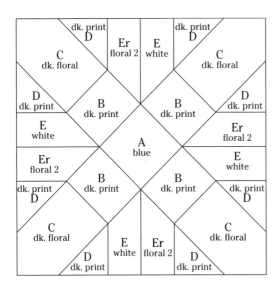

Dark Block

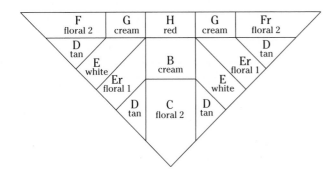

Side Triangle

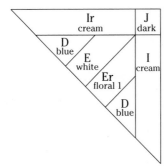

Corner Triangle

Border-2 Unit

- Following the Side and Corner Triangle Unit Assembly diagrams, make six side triangle units and four corner triangle units, using the same seam allowance width you used to make the blocks.

- As shown in the Quilt Assembly diagram (page 74) sew the blocks, side triangle units, and corner triangle units together in diagonal rows. Sew the rows together.

Borders

- To piece the border-2 strips, make 20 border units and sew them together, as shown in the Border Assembly diagram (page 74). Check the lengths of the strips with the quilt measurements and, if necessary, make adjustments in the seam allowances between the patches.

- Measure the pieced border strips and trim the border-1 strips to the correct lengths. Making sure that the red triangles point toward border 1, sew the long border-1 strips to the long border-2 strips. Repeat for the short strips. Sew the long border strips to the long sides of the quilt. Attach a corner square (M patch) to each end of the short border strips and sew them to the top and bottom of the quilt.

- Sew the long border-3 strips to the long sides of the quilt. Attach a corner square (N patch) to each end of the short strips. Sew the strips to the top and bottom of the quilt.

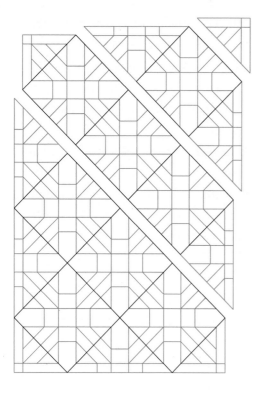

Quilt Assembly

Quilting and Finishing

- General instructions for layering, quilting, and binding begin on page 104. Refer to the Quilting Pattern diagram (Fig.3–21). Small Carpet is quilted in the ditch along the outside edges of the diagonal bands. The stitching lines cross at the pointer tips.

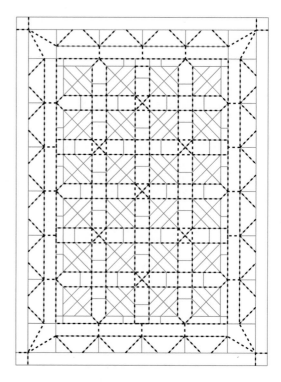

Quilting Pattern

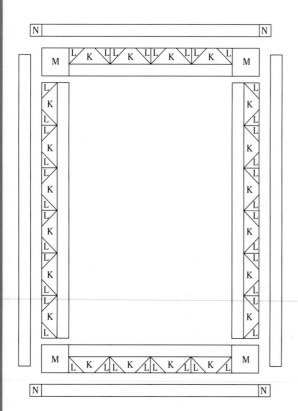

Border Assembly

Imagine
you were a carpet weaver in a previous life

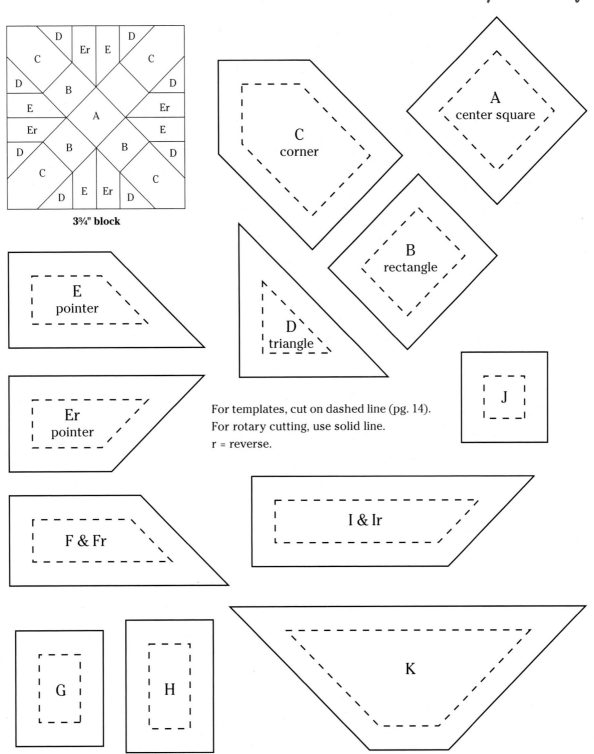

3¾" block

A — center square

C — corner

B — rectangle

E — pointer

Er — pointer

D — triangle

J

For templates, cut on dashed line (pg. 14).
For rotary cutting, use solid line.
r = reverse.

F & Fr

I & Ir

G

H

K

Imagine

*you were a carpet weaver
in a previous life*

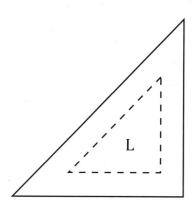

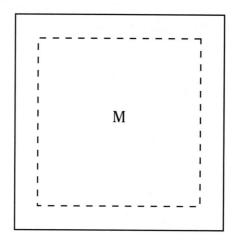

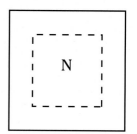

Drawing can be copied and enlarged for coloring.

One Block = Many Quilts   *Agnete Kay*

Imagine
you are an aquarellist

My third Aquarelle could not have been made without my having studied Deirdre Amsden's techniques. First, I tried making a colorwash quilt according to her excellent instructions, but the result was disappointing. My admiration for her skyrocketed.

Each patch in this block was cut from a different fabric, but all the blocks are the same. There are 25 well-chosen fabrics in every block, one for each patch. They include 5 dark fabrics, 4 medium ones, and the rest light. The colors used were black, purple, brown, yellow, blue, white, pink, and red. Who would have guessed that the result would appear so orderly, as if done in black and white.

Please note that the blocks do not have to be all the same. As long as you follow the zigzag pattern of lights and darks, the pattern will emerge. The quilt pattern given is slightly altered from the original for ease of construction.

AQUARELLE III, 36" x 56", 1995, by the author.

AQUARELLE III
Quilt 36" x 56"
12 Blocks 12" x 12"

Fabric Requirements
(based on 42"-wide fabric)

Fabrics	Yards	Pieces
Light Scraps	1⅝	24 B, 24 C, 72 D, 36 E, 36 Er
Medium Scraps	½	24 D, 12 E, 12 Er
Dark Scraps	¾	12 A, 24 B, 24 C
*Border	⅜	2 strips 4½" x 36½"
**Binding (pieced)		
	½	2 strips 1¾" x 59"
		2 strips 1¾" x 41"
Backing	1⅞	1 panel 40" x 61"
Batting		40" x 60"

*If you want the color of the borders to match a C patch in the block, as in Aquarelle III, cut the border strips and then cut 12 C patches from the remainder of the border fabric. Use these C patches to replace 12 of the light scrap C's.

**Binding yardage is based on the method described on page 106.

Assembly
Blocks
- Divide your scraps into lights, mediums, and darks.
- Cut border strips and set aside. Cut all the rest of the pieces as listed under Fabric Requirements. Template patterns for this quilt are provided on page 81–83.
- Following the Block Assembly diagram for color placement, make 12 blocks, all alike.
- Paying attention to the placement of the blocks to achieve the zigzag design, sew the blocks together in four rows of three (see Quilt Assembly, page 80). Then sew the rows together.

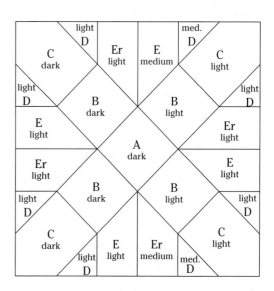

Block Assembly

Quilt Assembly

Borders

- The borders are extra long to allow for adjustments. Trim the border strips to fit the measurements of your quilt. Sew the border strips to the top and bottom.

Quilting and Finishing

- General instructions for layering, quilting, and binding can be found beginning on page 104. You can stitch in the ditch or outline quilt the blocks and the zigzags. The large triangles made from medium fabrics have been outline quilted (⅛" in from the seams) with black embroidery thread in an extra-large stitch (see Quilting Pattern diagram).

Outline Quilting Pattern

One Block = Many Quilts   *Agnete Kay*

Imagine
you are an aquarellist

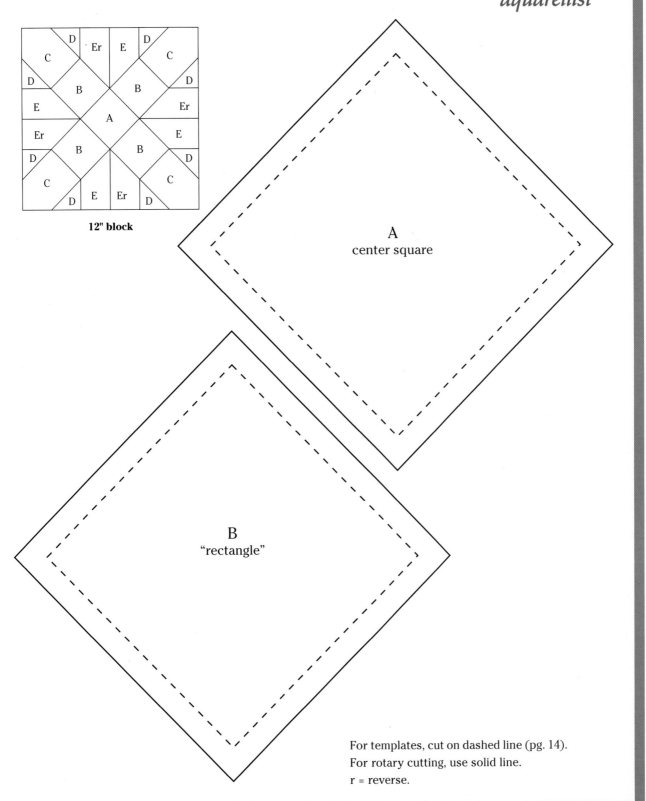

12" block

A
center square

B
"rectangle"

For templates, cut on dashed line (pg. 14).
For rotary cutting, use solid line.
r = reverse.

Imagine
you are an aquarellist

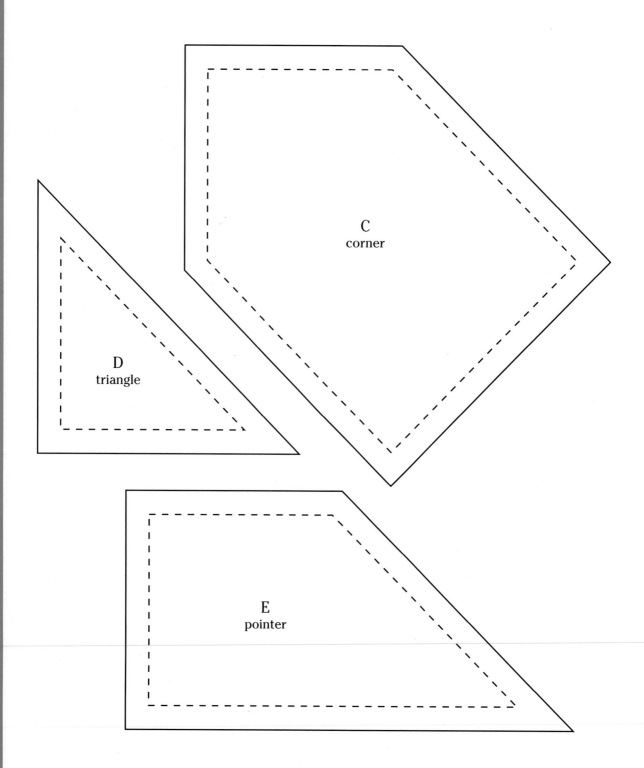

C
corner

D
triangle

E
pointer

One Block = Many Quilts   *Agnete Kay*

Imagine
you are an
aquarellist

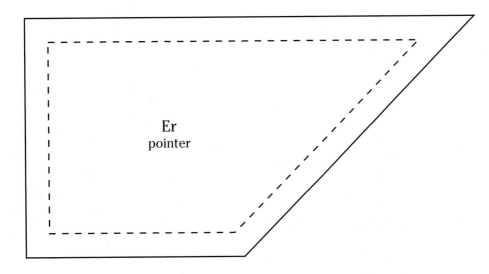

Er
pointer

Drawing can be enlarged for coloring.

Imagine
you are in the
Orient

Rich Oriental-looking color combinations, reminiscent of imperial ceremonial dress, were chosen for this quilt. Never be afraid of orange. It has made many an otherwise dull quilt interesting.

One Block = Many Quilts   *Agnete Kay*

The blocks are set with narrow sashing and tiny setting squares where the sashes meet. The border is made of dark fabric squares. Each border square is the same size as the IMAGINE BLOCK. The sashing continues out between the border blocks.

ORIENT, 44" x 44", 1995, by the author.

ORIENT

Quilt 44" x 44"

9 Blocks 8½" x 8½"

Fabric Requirements
(based on 42"-wide fabric)

Fabrics	Yards	Pieces
Lg. Blue & White Print	⅝	9 A, 36 C
Red Print	⅜	18 B, 36 D, 36 Er
Peach Print	⅜	18 B, 36 D, 36 E
Aqua Print	¼	12 strips 1¼" x 9"
Gold Print	⅛	8 strips 1¼" x 9"
		4 squares 1¼" x 1¼"
Black Print	1⅛	16 squares 9" x 9"
*Binding	¼	4 strips 1¾" x 26"
Backing	2⅞	2 panels 25" x 48"
Batting		48" x 48"

*Binding yardage is based on the method described on page 106.

Assembly

Blocks

- Cut all the patches as listed under Fabric Requirements. Template patterns for this quilt are provided on pages 88–89.

- Because color placement in the blocks is important for producing this design, you may want to arrange all of your patches on a flat surface before you begin sewing the blocks. Following the Block Assembly diagram for color and position, use continuous piecing, described on page 16, to sew the nine blocks.

- Referring to the Quilt Assembly diagram, join the blocks and sashing strips together in rows. Then sew the block rows and sashing rows together to complete the quilt.

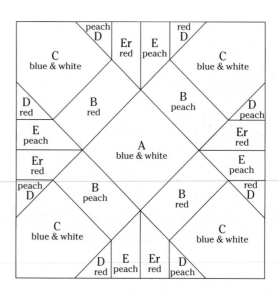

Block Assembly

Quilt Assembly

Quilting and Finishing

• In-the-ditch quilting outlines the sashing strips and the diagonal bands. A grid of quilting in red thread enhances the black border, as shown in the Quilting Pattern diagram. General instructions for layering, quilting, and binding begin on page 104.

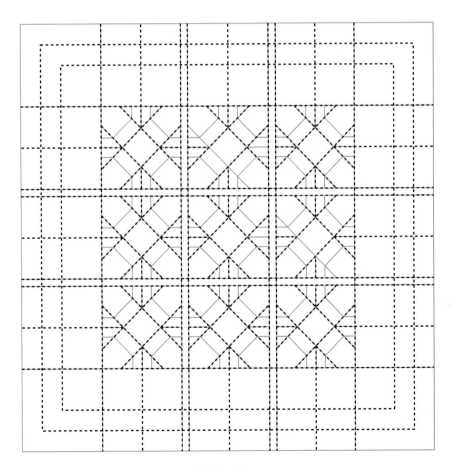

Quilting Pattern

Imagine you are in the Orient

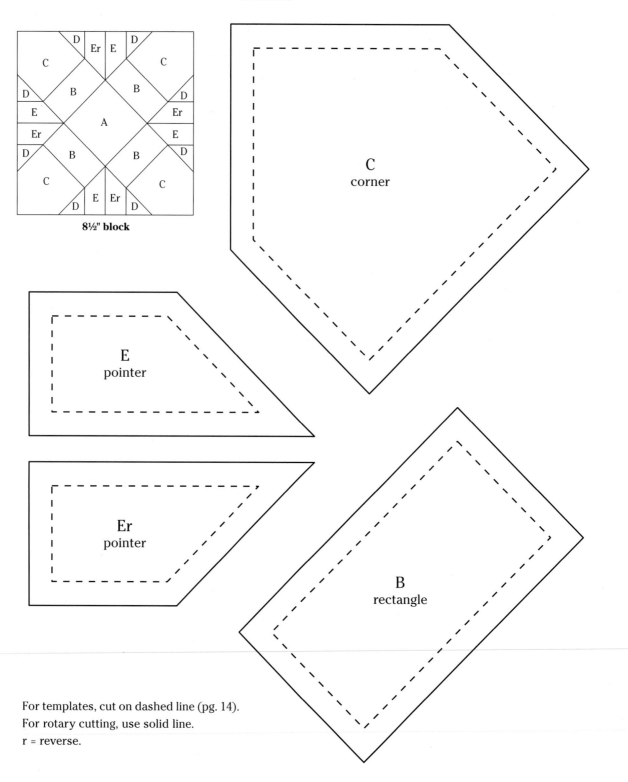

8½" block

C corner

E pointer

Er pointer

B rectangle

For templates, cut on dashed line (pg. 14).
For rotary cutting, use solid line.
r = reverse.

One Block = Many Quilts *Agnete Kay*

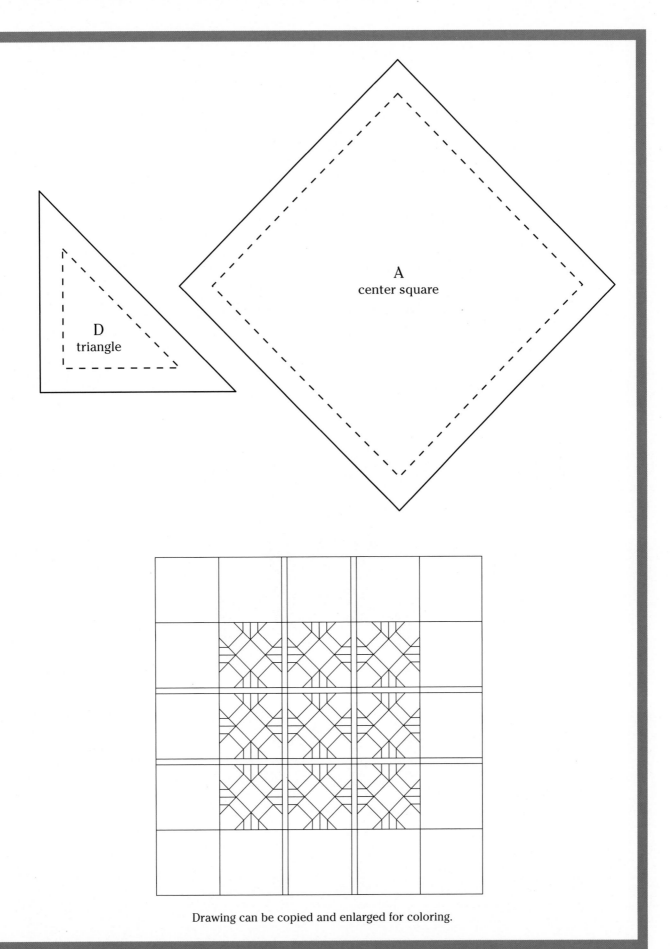

D
triangle

A
center square

Drawing can be copied and enlarged for coloring.

Imagine
you are in heaven

Heavenly though the piecing together of patches in endless variations of style and color may appear, I would not dare suggest that one could interpret heaven with cloth. But all the same, working with style and imagination in lovely fabrics must surely be a favorite occupation up there.

Having enough fabrics for a charm quilt, in which no two patches are cut from the same fabric, is pretty heavenly. With an IMAGINE BLOCK charm quilt, you may need to get all your fabrics out. A total of 25 different fabrics is needed for each block. Cutting and sorting each patch by color makes it easier to see if you have used a certain fabric before.

Some people like to store their fabric collection by color. I prefer to use the "sentimental filing system" in which I store fabrics together that go well together. I do, of course also have some bags labeled "solids," "blue scraps," "tree- and shrub-like prints," "expensive rarities," and so forth. My system suits me well. There is nothing inherently easier about remembering that yellows are in the third drawer to the right than remembering that the yellows are in the department-store bag.

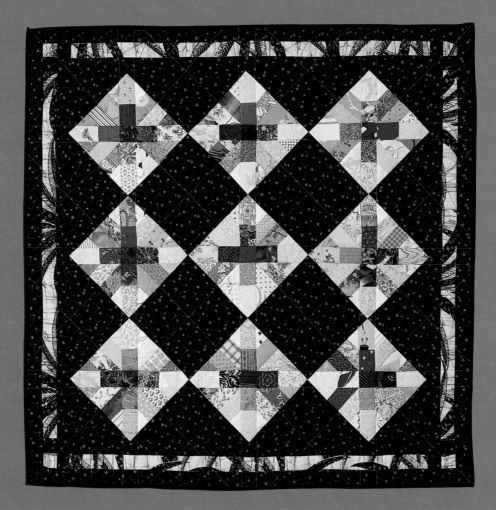

HEAVEN, 43" x 43", 1995, by the author.

Don't despair if you don't have enough, say, creams; just use gray instead. Or a pale purple will do for a pink. Rather than ruining your intended effect, it will probably make it all the more interesting. In some contexts, brown or gray can have a deadening effect on surrounding colors, so check it out first. But there is an advantage to adding brown to a quilt with many fierce pinks. Brown tones down the pinks and makes them appear dusty or, as it was known before, "old rose"…a lovely color.

It's a good idea to cut some extra patches of each color while you have the fabrics out. When I piece a charm quilt, I choose each new patch carefully before joining it to its neighbor. I want, as much as possible, to make each juxtaposition of fabrics sing with joy. Having some extra pieces helps near the end where the choices are dwindling. If you only have the exact number you need, you may be stuck with a very odd block, one in which none of the patches really go together.

In the quilt photo, you can see that the medium fabrics used for the A and B patches form a discernible cross in the center of each block. Notice that some of the B patches in the crosses disappear, and some of the pointers (E and Er patches) come forward, creating an interesting and mysterious quality to the design. To create this effect, for some or all of the blocks, cut a B patch from a light fabric and cut an E or Er from a medium fabric.

HEAVEN
Quilt 43" x 43"
9 Blocks 8" x 8"

Fabric Requirements
(based on 42"-wide fabric)

Fabrics	Yards	Pieces
*LIGHT SCRAPS	$\frac{7}{8}$	36 C, 72 D,
		36 E, 36 Er
*MEDIUM SCRAPS	$\frac{1}{4}$	9 A, 36 B
Large Print	$\frac{3}{8}$	
Border 2		4 strips 2" x 36",
		4 squares 2" x 2"
BLACK	$1\frac{1}{2}$	
Alternate Blocks		4 squares 8½" x 8½"
Side Triangles		2 squares 12⅝" x 12⅝"
Corner Triangles		2 squares 6⅝" x 6⅝"
Border 1		2 strips 2" x 39",
		2 strips 2" x 36"
Border 2		8 squares 2" x 2"
Border 3		2 strips 2" x 45",
		2 strips 2" x 42"
**Binding	$\frac{1}{2}$	4 strips 1¾" x 24"
Backing	$2\frac{3}{4}$	2 panels 24" x 47"
Batting		47" x 47"

*To make a charm quilt, no two scraps should be alike.

**Binding yardage is based on the method described on page 106.

Assembly

Blocks

- Cut the binding and border strips from the appropriate fabrics. (The yardage was figured based on cutting borders 1 and 3 parallel to the selvages.)
- Cut all the light and medium patches as listed under Fabric Requirements. Keep the lights and mediums separate. Template patterns for this quilt are provided on pages 95–96.
- Use continuous piecing, described on page 16, to sew the nine blocks.
- Refer to the Quilt Assembly diagram and join the pieced blocks, alternate blocks, and side triangles in diagonal rows. Sew the rows together, then add the corner triangles.

Borders

- Note – Borders are extra long to make fitting easier. Measure the quilt through the middle in both directions. Because the quilt is supposed to be square, there should be no more than a ⅛" discrepancy between the two measurements. (This is the maximum amount that can be eased while attaching the borders.) If the difference is larger than ⅛", you may want to make adjustments in the seam allowances between the blocks or the rows before adding the borders. After your adjustments have been made, measure the quilt again from top to bottom to find the side border length.
- For border 1, trim the two 36" strips to

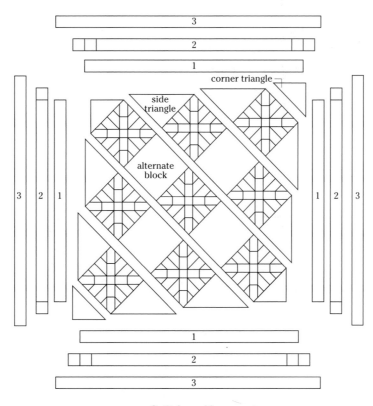

Quilt Assembly

the measurement for the side border length. Sew the strips to the sides of the quilt. Measure from side to side through the middle of the quilt, including the side borders. Cut the 39" border strips to that length and sew them to the top and bottom.

- For border 2, refer to the Quilt Assembly diagram (page 93). Use the same measurement for border 1 to trim the four large-print border strips. Sew a dark 2" square to each end of all four strips. Sew one of the strips to each side of the quilt. Sew a large-print 2" square to each end of the remaining two strips and sew these strips to the top and bottom of the quilt.

- For border 3, measure the quilt from top to bottom through the middle. Cut the 42" border strips to this length and sew them to the sides of the quilt. Measure from side to side through the middle and cut the 45" strips to this length. Sew them to the top and bottom to complete the quilt top.

Quilting and Finishing

- In-the-ditch quilting runs along both sides of the diagonal bands. Quilting lines also run from the pointers across the alternate blocks (see the Quilting Pattern diagram. General instructions for layering, quilting, and binding begin on page 104.

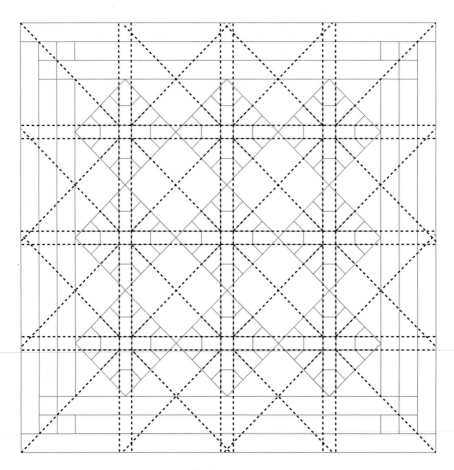

Quilting Pattern

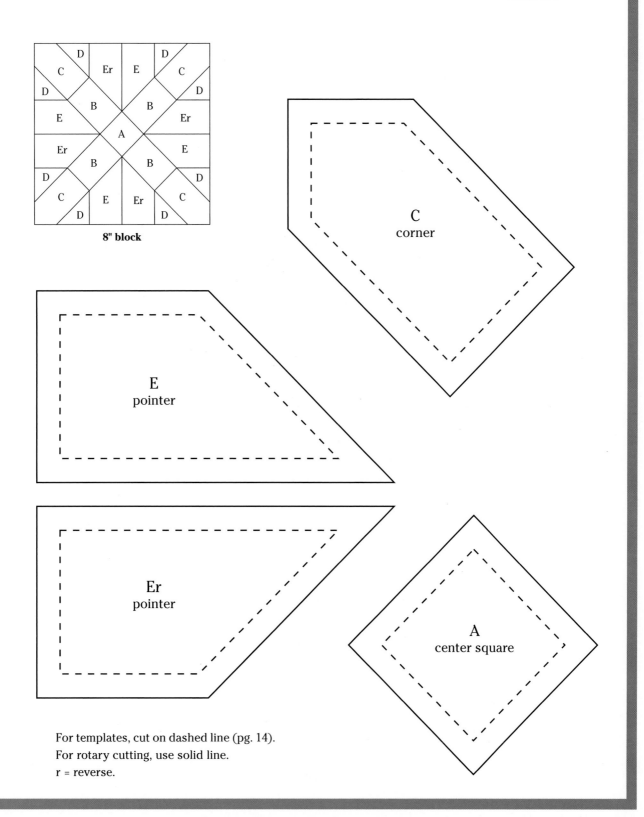

8" block

C
corner

E
pointer

Er
pointer

A
center square

For templates, cut on dashed line (pg. 14).
For rotary cutting, use solid line.
r = reverse.

Imagine you are in heaven

D
triangle

B
rectangle

12⅝"

12⅝"

side triangle

6⅝"

6⅝"

corner triangle

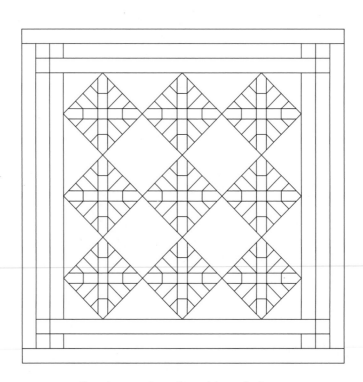

Drawing can be enlarged for coloring.

One Block = Many Quilts   *Agnete Kay*

Imagine it is Valentine's Day on Monday

...and you have nothing to give! For a quick heart design, you need only two special Imagine Blocks. The pointers are a little irregular, and the diagonal bands grow narrower toward the corners. The center square remains square.

Some of the piecing is a little tricky because the sewing cannot all be done along straight lines. All seams connected to the center square must stop at the penciled corner of each patch. Do not sew across the line into the seam allowance. Backstitch twice and cut the thread. Pin the pieced triangle units to the diagonal band as usual, but when stitching, just turn the fabric slightly (pivot with the needle down) when you get to the center square junctions and then continue the seam following the next pencil line. In the white space above the heart, a name or a message can be embroidered or written with indelible ink.

Play around with your design on graph paper and cardboard, then write the fabric names on each template. A tiny heart quilt makes a nice gift for a loved one. Of course, you can use any number of hearts to make a large quilt, two blocks per heart. The dark fan shapes in the corners will then become circles.

VALENTINE'S HEART, 12½" x 19", 1997, by the author.

VALENTINE
Quilt 12½" x 19"
2 Blocks 8½" x 8½"

Fabric Requirements
(based on 42"-wide fabric)

Fabrics	Yards	Pieces
Red Scraps	⅜	1 A, 4 B, 4 C, 2 D, 2 Dr, 2 E, 2 Er
Blue Scraps	¼	4 C, 4 D, 4 Dr
White Scraps	⅜	1 A, 4 B, 2 D, 2 Dr 6 E, 6 Er
White Border	¼	2 strips 2½" x 19½" 2 strips 1½" x 15"
*Binding	⅜	2 strips 1¾" x 21½" 2 strips 1¾" x 18"
Backing	1	1 panel 16½" x 23"
Batting		16½" x 23"

*Binding yardage is based on the method described on page 106. For rounded corners, you will need to use bias binding, which will require ⅝ yd. instead of ⅜ yd.

Assembly
Blocks

- Cut all the patches as listed under Fabric Requirements. Template patterns for this quilt are provided on pages 101–102.
- Because color placement is important for producing this design, you may want to arrange the patches on a flat surface before you begin sewing the blocks. Following the Block Assembly diagrams for color and position, use continuous piecing, described on page 16, to sew the two blocks.
- Join the blocks to form the heart.

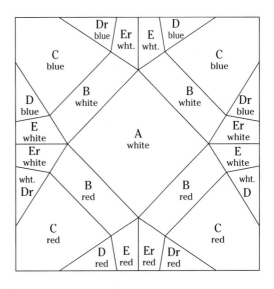

Top of Heart

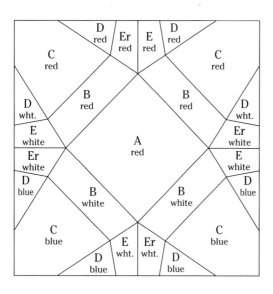

Bottom of Heart

Borders

- The borders have extra length to allow for adjustments. Sew the 2½"-wide borders to the sides of the quilt and trim the extra border length even with the raw quilt edges (Quilt Assembly diagram). Sew the 1½"-wide borders to the top and bottom of the quilt and trim the extra length.

Quilting and Finishing

- In-the-ditch quilting follows the heart shape and outlines the corner shapes (see the Quilting Pattern diagram). General instructions for layering and quilting begin on page 104.
- If you want your quilt to have square corners, follow the binding directions on page 106. If you prefer rounded corners, see Rounded Corners, page 110.

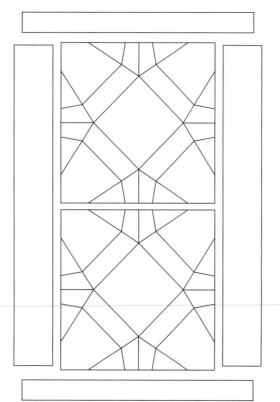

Quilt Assembly

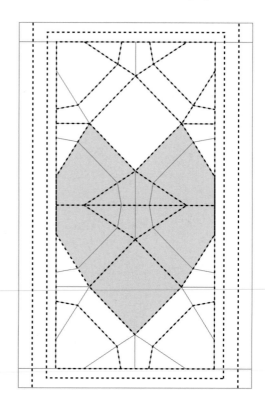

Quilting Pattern

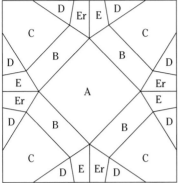

8½" block

E
pointer

Er
pointer

A
center square

For templates, cut on dashed line (pg. 14).
For rotary cutting, use solid line.
r = reverse.

Imagine
it is
Valentine's Day
on Monday

C
corner

B
rectangle

D
triangle

Dr
triangle

Drawing can be enlarged for coloring.

One Block = Many Quilts   *Agnete Kay*

CHAPTER 4

Imagine
the
Finishing
Touches

F or once, a quilt turned out exactly as I had hoped. Rarely are my finished quilts the lovely pieces I saw in my mind's eye when I began them. It is so exciting when it happens. Lunch is forgotten. Time stands still.

Labeling

When you have finished your quilt top, it's time to name and sign your quilt. You can write the name of the quilt on the front near the bottom, either next to or opposite your signature or initials. Include the date. This front label can be embroidered or written with an indelible pen.

When the quilt is finished, you can add a label on the back with more details, such as your address, what inspired the design, and whether it was accepted into a show, or whatever else you would like. Remember, those details are written for your own satisfaction and maybe for your offspring. Also, as some quilters suggest, every quilt is an unequalled record of history and deserves all the documentation and preservation it can get.

Layering

For backing, you will need a piece of cotton fabric (pieced from left-overs or purchased new) at least 4" wider and longer than your quilt top. Lay out your well-ironed backing, right side down, on a carpet or table. Stretch and smooth it thoroughly. If you are working on the floor, you can pin it to the carpet. On top of the backing, lay the batting, which should be the same size as the backing. Smooth, but do not stretch the batting. Then add the finished quilt top, right side up. Smooth the top from the center toward the edges.

Pin the three layers together, starting in the middle and working your way out toward the edges. It can be quite a workout crawling around on all fours on the floor. If you use safety pins, then you are

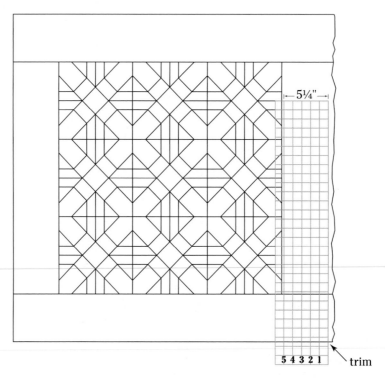

Fig. 4–1

all done in one go. For a large quilt, thread basting will hold the layers securely. Basting is best begun in the middle, working outward in a spiral. Some quilters prefer basting in a grid pattern.

Next, trim the edges of the quilt by aligning one of the lines in your ruler with a border or block seam. For example, if your quilt has a 5" border, align the 5¼" (includes seam allowance) ruler line with the border seam. (Fig. 4–1). Trim only enough to even the edges of the quilt and remove the frayed edges. If there are pieced seams at the edges of the quilt instead of a border strip, be careful to leave a sufficient seam allowance as you trim. You can mark the trim line with a pencil for cutting with scissors, or you can use a rotary cutter to trim the edges.

Stay-stitch the layers close to the edge (approximately ¹⁄₁₆" or 2 mm) all around the quilt. To keep from stretching the edges while stay-stitching, you can use your fingers to help feed the quilt toward the needle as you sew.

Quilting

Quilting stitches keep the top, batting, and backing together. Unlikely as it seems, the color of the quilting thread is important. The thread can be neutral, of course, or matching, but a contrasting color can work wonders. Once, I made a quilt top that looked rather dull. I decided to quilt it with bright pink thread, and the difference in the general appearance was remarkable. Just that little bit of bright pink was enough to make it sparkle.

Most of my IMAGINE BLOCK quilts are machine quilted. Some quilts in this book are hand quilted, mostly with perle cotton. Quilting designs, homemade or bought, can be traced on the quilt top with a marker that will wash out.

Machine quilting

For machine quilting, I often use a simple quilting pattern of all-over, one-way parallel lines. Sometimes, I quilt a grid in the ditch, stitching in the seam along the side of a patch or a block.

For a quilting pattern with a "tartan" look, start by quilting diagonally from corner to corner across the quilt, in both directions (Fig. 4–2a, page 106). Next, stitch a line on both sides of each diagonal. The lines should all be the same distance from the diagonals, perhaps the width of a 3" ruler. Stitch four more lines, but this time at a greater distance, say double the ruler width (Fig. 4–2b, page 106). Continue in this way with varying distances for each set of lines. Make sure that, for every line you sew, there is another parallel line on the other half of the quilt, and two more lines the same distance apart but running in the opposite direction. This quilting pattern suits many quilts, and it is quite easy to sew (Fig. 4–2c, page 106).

I like to mark quilting lines by drawing a pin along a ruler. If you draw a lot of pin lines, some of them may disappear by the time you sew two or three. The best thing is to draw one or two lines, sew them, then draw another line or two. It may seem impractical to have to stop to mark so often, but since neck pains and sore

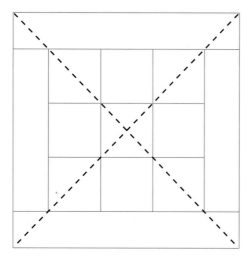

Fig. 4–2a

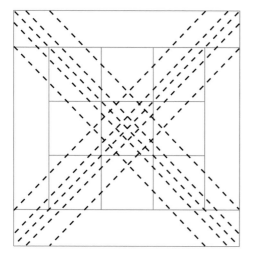

Fig. 4–2b

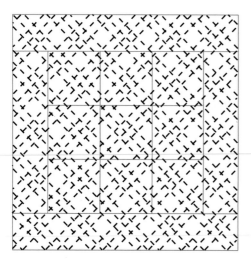

Fig. 4–2c

shoulders frequently accompany machine quilting, it is actually an excellent idea to stand up occasionally and give your body a rest.

Hand quilting

For hand quilting, use quilting thread and a between quilting needle. To begin and end a row of stitches, tie a small knot in one end of the thread. Gently tug the knot until it pops through the top and is hidden in the batting. The quilting stitches, in addition to holding the layers together, also add a pattern of shadows to the finished top, so bear that in mind. If, like me, you have difficulty making very tiny stitches, try using thicker thread (perle cotton), a larger needle, larger stitches, and a larger pattern. The quilting will look graphic and attractive with the highly visible thread, bold as brass, contrasting with the fabric of the pieced blocks. Quilting frames or hoops are preferred by many, but I use neither.

Binding

When the quilting is done, it's time for binding, and the choice of binding fabric is much more important than it seems at first glance. The binding can be neutral, but more likely, you will want a fabric that creates a suitable frame around your quilt and adds a feeling of completion. You can also choose a fabric that picks up a color from an accent fabric in your blocks. Such a binding may add great interest to the finished work, so choose your binding fabric with care.

To audition a fabric for binding, fold

the fabric to resemble a long border strip and lay the quilt top on the folded fabric so that only a portion (the width of a binding strip) shows. This test can often surprise you, inasmuch as what you thought would match doesn't, and what you thought was way off the mark is both exciting and suitable.

Because the average useable width of fabric from the bolt is 42", binding strips that are as short or shorter than 42" can be cut from selvage to selvage. Strips longer than 42" can be cut parallel to the selvage, or pieced to conserve fabric. Cut or piece four strips the width and length given in your pattern's Fabric Requirements section. The cut binding strips have some extra length to allow for custom fitting. Trim two of the strips to the length of your quilt as measured through the middle (Fig. 4–3). If the quilt edges are slightly shorter or longer than the middle measurement, the binding can be eased to fit.

Place one of the long strips on the side of the quilt top, right sides together, aligning the raw edge of the strip with the raw edge of the quilt. Pin in place. Use a sewing machine to stitch ¼" (unless otherwise indicated) from the raw edge (Fig. 4–4, page 108). If the layers aren't feeding evenly, you may need to use a walking foot. Remove the pins as you sew. Finger press the binding to the outside of the quilt (Fig. 4–5, page 108). Repeat for the other long side of the quilt.

For the top and bottom of the quilt, measure the width of the quilt through the

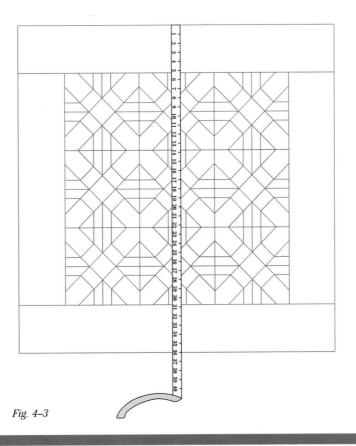

Fig. 4–3

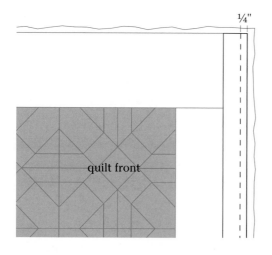

Fig. 4–4

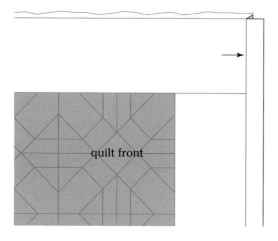

Fig. 4–5

middle including the two strips already sewn (Fig. 4–6). Cut the remaining strips to that length. Pin and stitch the strips to the top and bottom of the quilt.

Turn your quilt backing side up. The binding will be sticking out, wrong side up, around all four sides. Fold the binding inward all around so the cut binding edge nearly touches the quilt edges (Fig. 4–7). Press the folds. Turn the folded binding around the quilt's edges, fitting it snugly and evenly (Fig. 4–8). Press this new fold lightly only at the corners.

Open the folds at the corners and, using the folds as guidelines (Fig. 4–9), cut off the triangle to reduce bulk in the corner. Refold the corner down as shown in Fig 4–10.

Refold the binding, forming a miter in each corner (Fig. 4–11). Pin the binding in place every 2" to 3" (10 to 15 cm), making sure your binding is the same width on the front all the way around. You can judge the width by eye.

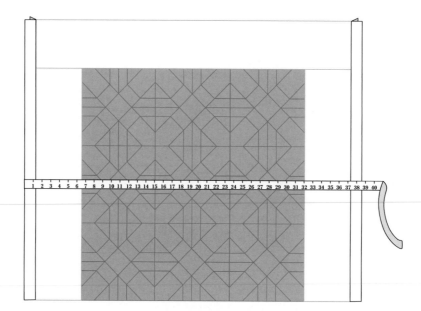

Fig. 4–6

One Block = Many Quilts   *Agnete Kay*

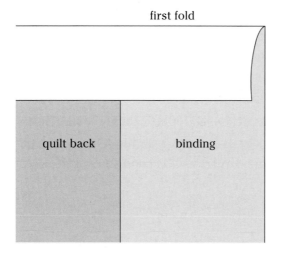

Fig. 4–7

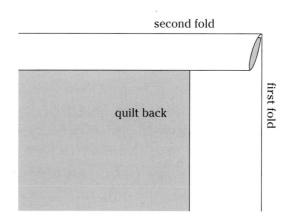

Fig. 4–8

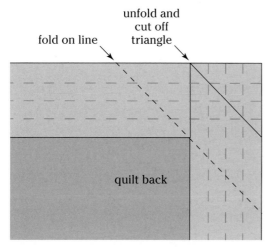

Fig. 4–9

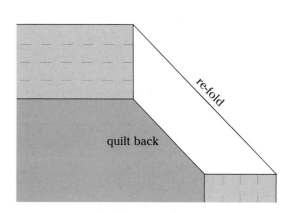

Fig. 4–10

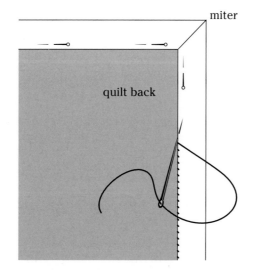

Fig. 4–11

Hand sew the binding to the backing with small tight blind stitches, making sure not to stitch through the front of the quilt. Remove pins as you go.

If you would rather finish the binding by machine instead of by hand, you can machine stitch the binding to the back of the quilt first, then turn it to the front. Machine stitch very close to the folded edge from the top of the quilt. This method, while quicker, leaves a visible seam on the back you may not want. Snip any loose thread ends and remove the basting threads or safety pins.

Rounded Corners

Use a round object, such as a drinking glass, as a pattern for marking and cutting the corners.

For the binding to lie flat, you need to use continuous bias binding, which is made as follows:

Cut 2" wide strips on the bias (45° angle), as shown in Fig. 4–12.

Sew the strips together at a 45° angle (Fig. 4–13) to make one long, continuous strip.

On the starting end of the continuous strip, turn under ¼". Start on a side of the quilt, not a corner, and leave at least 3" of binding strip free for finishing the ends (Fig. 4–14). Beginning with a backstitch, sew the binding to the quilt with a ¼" seam allowance. Ease the binding around the corners as you sew.

Stop sewing a couple of inches before the starting place and backstitch. Remove the quilt from the sewing machine and clip the threads. Cut off the end of the strip so

it overlaps the beginning end by about ½". Smooth the strip in place and finish sewing the binding in place (Fig. 4–15).

Turn the binding to the back and sew, as described for straight-grain binding on page 106. Again ease the binding around the corners as you hand-stitch it in place.

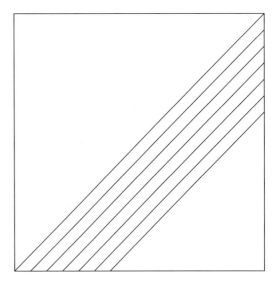

Fig. 4–12

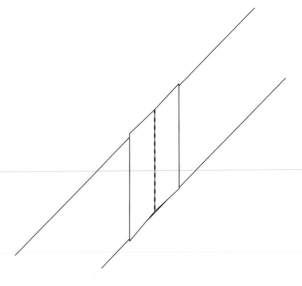

Fig. 4–13

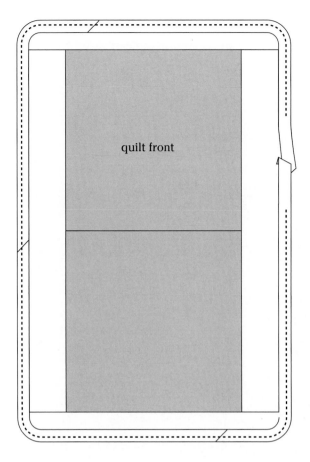

Fig. 4–14

Hanging Sleeve

If the quilt is to be hung on a wall, you can sew a sleeve on the back to hold a stick or rod for hanging. Refer to Fig. 4–16. To make a sleeve, cut or piece an 8" (20 cm) wide strip that is as long as the quilt is wide. Sew a ¼" hem (twofolds) on each end of the strip. Press the strip in half lengthwise, wrong sides together. Using a ¼" seam allowance, sew the long edges together to form a tube. Press the tube so that the seam will be on the back. Hand stitch the top and bottom edges of the tube to the backing, but be careful that the stitching doesn't come through to the front.

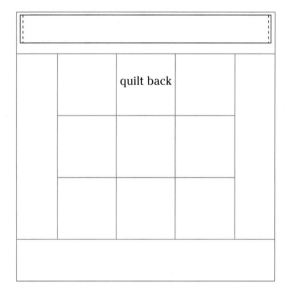

Fig. 4–16

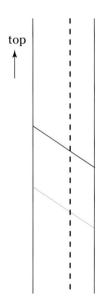

Fig. 4–15

LEIGHTON QUILT, 35" x 35", 1995, by the author. Tiles and quilt blocks have a lot in common, and anyone interested in either should visit the Leighton House in London where Lord Leighton's breathtaking collection of antique Islamic ceramic tiles is displayed. The memory of London and the Leighton House, with its brilliant blue and turquoise tiles, inspired me to make some tile-like arrangements of the IMAGINE BLOCK.

The Gallery

*I*n school, I never liked mathematics, with the exception of geometry, which came easy to me and which was almost fun. Art was always interesting. It was called "drawing" in my time. One year, perhaps grade five, the drawing teacher handed out graph paper to the class and instructed us to design as many pattern variations as we could, with each variation fitting into a 4" square. He showed us the eight-point star but told us not to limit ourselves to stars. Looking back on it, I realize that, though the teacher had probably never even seen a quilt, he was in effect teaching us about quilt blocks. For me, they were the most fun drawing classes we ever had, and I was sorry when we had to move on to other subjects.

TRIP AROUND THE MAYPOLE, 57" x 57", 1998, by the author. With this quilt, I wanted a dynamic placement of the colors of the rainbow. Once finished, it reminded me of a satellite photo – blue water, green forests, plains, and the red-hot cities of the world where we live.

One Block = Many Quilts   *Agnete Kay*

LITTLE COPENHAGEN, 16" x 20", 1997, by the author. Imagine the City of the Beautiful Towers. Climb one and survey a pieced pattern of red-fired tiles and copper roofs, mixed with red brick, sandstone, and yellow ochre. Copenhagen holds a secret. Walk its narrow streets with your loved one and magic happens. There, in the King's Copenhagen, I misspent my youth, absorbing its unique history, architecture, and geography. This quilt won second place in the doll quilt category at the 1997 Calgary Stampede.

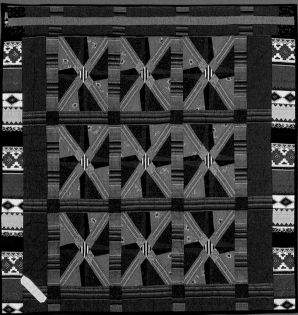

ALBERTA ATHABASCA ROSE, 49" x 49", 1997, and back of quilt, by the author. For me, the beadwork designs of the Plains Indians are full of glory, allegory, and sorrow. They are an endless source of inspiration. I made this quilt during the 1997 Stampede in Calgary, Alberta. The central area consists of four IMAGINE BLOCKS in typical beadwork colors. A reverse appliqué rose, in a style similar to one used by Tsuu T'ina bead workers, covers the middle. The emblem of Alberta is the deep pink, wild rose, and Calgary's nearest neighbors are the Tsuu T'ina people, who are members of the Athabasca language group.

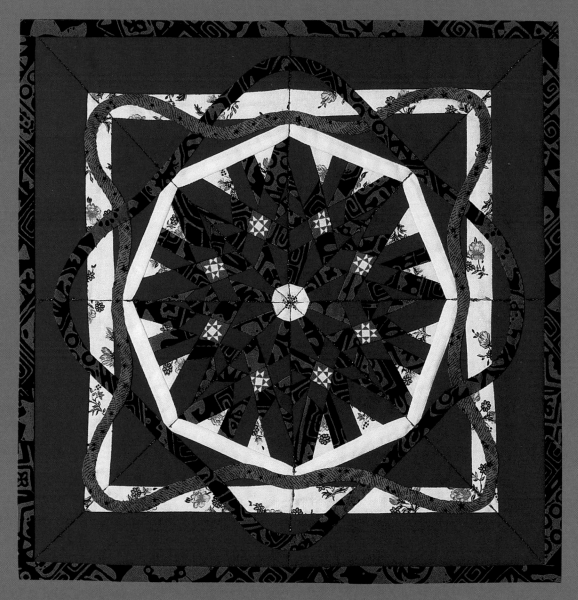

HEAVENLY BODIES, 13" x 13", 1997, by the author. With this quilt, I remember Hale-Bopp, the beautiful comet. Many evenings I watched it from our front door as it floated low on the northwest sky.

...AND HERE WE LIVED FOR MANY YEARS, 33" x 44", 1997, by the author. This quilt was a finalist in the Shelburne Museum's Quilting a Legacy contest. I decided to make a picture of our house we have owned since 1981. At the time I made this quilt, two sons had left home, leaving only our daughter. So, in the new and relative quiet, the busy childhood home had suddenly become an unreachable past, a memory, and an image behind an impenetrable web. In the quilt, the web is represented by a grid, made up of diagonal bands and pointers.

One Block = Many Quilts   *Agnete Kay*

READING LIST

Amsden, Deirdre. *Colorwash Quilts*, That Patchwork Place 1994.

Crow, Nancy. *Nancy Crow: Work in Transition*, AQS 1992.

Gutcheon, Beth. *Perfect Patchwork Primer*, Penguin Books 1981.

Hughes, Robert. *Amish: The Art of the Quilt*, Knopf 1990.

Pottinger, David. *Quilts from the Indiana Amish*, Dutton 1983.

Rae, Janet. *The Quilts of the British Isles*, Dutton 1987.

AQUARELLE II, 47" x 47", 1995, by the author. Making the second aquarelle quilt was as natural as breathing. (AQUARELLE I is on page 8.) I saw a blue fabric with soccer balls on it, and straight away it reminded me of my favorite team, Leeds United F.C. Their colors are white and blue, with yellow as the alternative jersey color. I call the quilt IT'S IN THE NET! It looks very different when viewed from various distances. The quilt has 16 soccer balls, one in each center square. The net is formed by the light corner and rectangle patches, and the dark background is formed by well-blended greens and blues with one orange for an accent. A simple border was cut from a dark green print.

AQS Books on Quilts

This is only a partial listing of the books available from the American Quilter's Society. AQS books are known worldwide for timely topics, clear writing, beautiful color photos, and accurate illustrations and patterns. The following books are available from your local bookseller, quilt shop, or public library. If you are unable to locate certain titles in your area, you may order by mail from the AMERICAN QUILTER'S SOCIETY, P.O. Box 3290, Paducah, KY 42002-3290. Add $2.00 for postage for the first book ordered and 40¢ for each additional book. Include item number, title, and price when ordering. Allow 14 to 21 days for delivery. Customers with Visa, MasterCard, or Discover may phone in orders from 7:00–5:00 CST, Mon.–Fri., 1-800-626-5420.